GOLDEN GLOW

GOLDEN GLOW

HOW KAITLIN SANDENO ACHIEVED GOLD IN THE POOL AND IN LIFE

Dan D'Addona
Kaitlin Sandeno

ROWMAN & LITTLEFIELD
Lanham • Boulder • New York • London

Published by Rowman & Littlefield
An imprint of The Rowman & Littlefield Publishing Group, Inc.
4501 Forbes Boulevard, Suite 200, Lanham, Maryland 20706
www.rowman.com

6 Tinworth Street, London, SE11 5AL, United Kingdom

British Library Cataloguing in Publication Information Available

Library of Congress Cataloging-in-Publication Data

Names: D'Addona, Dan, 1981– author. | Sandeno, Kaitlin, 1983– author.
Title: Golden glow : how Kaitlin Sandeno achieved Gold in the pool and in life / Dan
    D'Addona, Kaitlin Sandeno.
Description: Lanham, Maryland : ROWMAN & LITTLEFIELD, [2019] | Includes
    bibliographical references.
Identifiers: LCCN 2018057282 (print) | LCCN 2019002463 (ebook) | ISBN
    9781538117040 (electronic) | ISBN 9781538117033 | ISBN 9781538117033
    (cloth : alk. paper)
Subjects: LCSH: Sandeno, Kaitlin, 1983–Juvenile literature. | Women swimmers—
    United States—Biography—Juvenile literature. | Swimmers—United States—
    Biography—Juvenile literature. | Athletes—Conduct of life—Juvenile literature. |
    Olympic Games (27th : 2000 : Sydney, N.S.W.)—Juvenile literature. | Olympic
    Games (28th : 2004 : Athens, Greece)—Juvenile literature.
Classification: LCC GV838 (ebook) | LCC GV838 .D328 2019 (print) | DDC
    796.812092 [B] —dc23
LC record available at https://lccn.loc.gov/2018057282

♾™ The paper used in this publication meets the minimum requirements of American
National Standard for Information Sciences—Permanence of Paper for Printed Library
Materials, ANSI/NISO Z39.48-1992.

Printed in the United States of America

CONTENTS

ACKNOWLEDGMENTS

This book would not have been possible without the help and support of many people, beginning with my family. Thank you to my wonderful wife, Corene, and my daughters, Lena and Mara, for their support in writing this book—and in every aspect of life. They are constant inspirations in my life.

I want to thank the staff at Rowman & Littlefield for taking on this project, particularly Christen Karniski, who was supportive from the beginning and was a pleasure to work with, starting from our days running into one another at baseball conferences.

Many thanks to Emily White, Kaitlin's manager, who was also instrumental in putting this project together. I have never met a manager so involved and personable as Emily, and that made the process infinitely easier and comfortable.

A huge thank you to everyone who helped shape Kaitlin's story, from coach to friend to family. Coaches Vic and Renee Riggs, Jon Urbanchek, and Mark Schubert shed a lot of light on Kaitlin's swimming, as well as her personality and character, at different times in her life, helping to bring the total scope to fruition.

Kaitlin also had plenty of teammates from every level of her life eager to talk about what it was like to swim with her and what kind of person she was outside of the pool. So big thanks to Amy Walloch, Kammy Miller, Bree Deters, Rachael Waller, Lindsay Mintenko, Diana Munz, and Natalie Coughlin for taking the time to talk about the impact Kaitlin had on them and the bond they were able to share as youth teammates, Olympic teammates, and everything in between.

It wasn't only teammates who helped with this project, either. Erik Rees and Cory Tomlinson of the Jessie Rees Foundation provided a different perspective on Kaitlin's role with the foundation and her motivation out of the pool.

Without them, the well-rounded version of Kaitlin would not have been so crystal clear.

This book would not have been possible without the amazing photography of Peter H. Bick, who has been the premier swimming photographer for decades. Thank you for being an awesome photographer and colleague, and a great friend. Thanks to my *Swimming World* crew for all of the support. Also, a huge thank you to Summer Sanders, who provided a unique perspective as a fellow swimmer who went into television and hosted many of the shows Kaitlin now hosts. And thanks to Ella Eastin for providing some insight into what Kaitlin was like as a swimming instructor—yet another layer to her post-swimming career.

To Kaitlin's family: Thank you so much for welcoming me into your homes, pools, and lives to support this project. Thank you for the stories, photographs, memories, and genuine support. Without you—Jill, Tom, Pete, Camlyn, Amy, Steve, Mike—this project would have never become what it is today. Your love for and support of Kaitlin has proved to be unwavering. Thank you so much for adding me into that wave of support.

And finally, to Kaitlin: Thank you for taking a chance on a writer with big ambitions in the sport of swimming. The instant connection, or reconnection, we had made this book possible. I have enjoyed every second of getting to know you and, during this process, have seen our relationship transform from source to colleague to friend, and I cherish that. Thank you for letting me help tell your amazing story.

—Dan D'Addona

For so long, sharing my story was on my bucket list. Dan D'Addona allowed me to check off that box. From the bottom of my heart, thank you for making this dream come true. To my manager, Emily White, you completed our dream team and for that I am so grateful. Thank you to Rowman & Littlefield for taking a chance on us and allowing us to share my story in hopes of inspiring, encouraging, and motivating others.

I am seldom speechless but tend to be when trying to find the right words to thank my mom, dad, and sisters. You are my everything. I thank God that I can call you my family. To the moon, forever and always. I dedicate this book to you. Steve and Mike, I could not have asked for better brother-in-laws or husbands for my sisters. Thank you for joining this wild ride with the Sandenos as my brothers.

ACKNOWLEDGMENTS

Michael, Thomas, Sarah, Luke, Max, and James—I am so proud to be your aunt. It has been such a joy watching each of you grow and mature. I pray you live your dreams and find true happiness. Being your aunt is one of my favorite roles in life.

To my Hogan family—Tom, Mimi, and Jack—there's no other way to put it: I totally scored with you. What an Irish blessing to marry into your wonderful family.

To all my coaches, I am forever indebted. I am honored to have swum for you. The times we shared are priceless, and the journey we had is surreal. Thank you for never giving up on me. I could not have done it without you.

To the Rees family, I can never express my gratitude for allowing me to take part in Jessie's dream to encourage every child fighting cancer to NEGU. Her mission and your faith in me shaped my life when I was lost. You have helped and encouraged so many people, and I am blessed to have been one of them.

To my core—Amy, Bree, Cory, Kammy, and Rachael—I could not be any luckier to have the best tribe of friends. Thank you for your support throughout the years and for doing life with me. I cherish the friendship, memories, tears, and laughter we have shared. To my teammates and medical/wellness team throughout the years, whether you know it or not, you made me better. And I thank you for that.

To my Olympic roomie and bestie, Diana—dang did we have some fun! Our memories will forever keep an unbreakable bond between us. I could not have asked for a better human being to share it with.

I will always feel an alliance with El Toro High School, the University of Southern California, USA Swimming, and the University of Michigan. Thank you for providing opportunities that allowed me to live this incredible journey.

Finally, to my husband, Peter Joseph Hogan, you are an answer to my prayers. You are the best thing to ever happen to me. I love you for not only who you are, but also who I am when I am with you. Your support, love, encouragement, and sense of humor make my heart smile. Thank you for loving me for who I am. You are mine and I am yours until Heaven is our home.

—Kaitlin Sandeno

INTRODUCTION

Kaitlin Sandeno touched the wall and looked up. With hope in her eyes, the 17-year-old Olympic swimmer found her name on the scoreboard and the number "4" next to it. That hope quickly faded away as Kaitlin tried to wrap her head around what had just happened. It was the 2000 Olympic Games in Sydney, Australia, and this teen phenom from California had just finished one spot away from medaling.

She was crushed.

Of course Kaitlin had wanted to win a medal at the Olympics—gold preferred—as any world-class athlete would strive for, but this was different. Kaitlin had overheard plenty of medal talk leading up to the games, then in the Olympic Village as the games began. She was the first shot at a medal for the United States, as the 400-meter individual medley is traditionally one of the first events of the games. Plus, she was lining up against Ukraine's Yana Klochkova, the best in the world.

All of that medal talk got to Kaitlin. It was something that had never happened before. She had never been so visibly crushed after a defeat. But that was a turning point for Kaitlin. She would never be that crushed again, no matter what happened in the pool. She vowed to never let the talk of others get into her head again—and to find the silver lining in every situation and make that her gold.

Sometimes, that silver lining—and gold—is literal. Four years later, Kaitlin was back in the Olympics in Athens in the same situation. And again, she was going head-to-head with Yana in the finals. This time, she hung with Yana the entire race, and the two touched the wall together. Yana won the race by a mere tenth of a second, but it was Kaitlin, getting silver, who began to celebrate like she had won. She jumped up, yelled, and was so animated that people were afraid that she misread the scoreboard and thought she had won the race. But Kaitlin knew she had the number "2" next to her name. After learning from her experience in the 2000 Olympics, Kaitlin was focused on her time and not so much her place. She could not control how fast everyone else swam. She could only control her own lane. Kaitlin didn't care that she won the silver medal, barely missing gold. She was thrilled because in a race of that magnitude, she was somehow able to drop six seconds from her previous best time. Now, the 400 IM is not a sprint, but it is far from a race like the mile, which typically sees time drops like that. This was one of the biggest and most stunning time drops in the history of swimming. Six seconds from the Olympic trials to the Olympics is unheard of, until Kaitlin raced her 400 IM in 2004. Unlike four years prior, where the situation crushed her, this time, she crushed it with the right outlook and a stunning performance.

Even though Kaitlin would go on to win Olympic gold on a relay, a relay that took down a world record, she maintains that her silver medal in the 400 IM in Athens was her gold. It was her moment. The one where she proved to herself what she was truly capable of in the water. It was a life lesson that she lived and took with her into every aspect of her life.

Many people view a silver lining as a negative thing, but Kaitlin has embraced it as life's plan. Things don't always go perfectly, and how people handle the disappointments and pain is what shapes them. It is not an easy thing to bounce back from hurt or heartache, but Kaitlin proved to herself in Athens that she can do it. She has spent most of her post-swimming life proving to others that they can do it as the national spokesperson for the Jessie Rees Foundation.

The life of Jessie Rees is a silver lining in itself. Jessie was a brave kid battling cancer, but she didn't let that battle end, even in death. Her idea of spreading joy to children with cancer through hospital visits and handing out JoyJars has become her legacy, a legacy that has helped bring a little joy to thousands of children throughout the country. That is Jessie's gold.

That is quite a silver lining, something that drew Kaitlin to Jessie and, eventually, to the foundation. It is a perfect match. No one can inspire others to find their silver lining unless they have found it themselves. This is the story of how Kaitlin found hers and continues to inspire others to find their own silver lining—and change it to gold.

MONUMENTAL MEETING

It was just a quick meeting, but while the interaction lasted just a few moments, the impact was lasting for Kaitlin Sandeno. The retired Olympic swimmer took one look at Jessie Rees and fell in love. Here was this young kid fighting to live, yet doing everything she could to help other kids with cancer. Kaitlin couldn't help but be captivated by her story and her spirit—and it was the only time they would ever meet. Kaitlin has met many people in her life who have helped shape her—as a child, a woman, a swimmer, a speaker, and an activist—but this meeting with Jessie was nothing short of life changing.

"This all came about while I was coaching at Sandeno Swim Club, a program my sister Camlyn and I started to promote health, fitness, exercise, and swim technique," said Kaitlin.

One of the moms on my team asked me if I had heard about this little girl with two inoperable brain tumors on the Mission Viejo Nadadores club and if there was anything I could sign to give to her as encouragement. I found one of my old national team warm-up jackets and signed it to have it given to her. Then I found out about a fundraiser to help her family with all the medical bills. It was similar to a swim-a-thon at a local private high school. I rallied a few other Olympians and national team swimmers to attend with me, and that is where I first met Jessie and her family.

When we met her, she was really frail. She was in a wheelchair. She was wearing a huge, baggy sweatshirt with the first Jessie Rees Foundation logo. She had one of those medical masks on and glasses that blurred her vision because the doctors thought that would help with one of the tumors. That was my one and only time interacting with her. I remember when I met Erik, Jessie's dad. He had these huge blue eyes, and they were so full of sorrow. That was my first experience looking into someone's eyes and seeing so much pain. I just wanted to do something. I felt so helpless. I continued to follow her story.

While she was going through her own treatment, Jessie, along with the help of her parents, had started giving JoyJars to kids with cancer. The jars are hand packed with fun toys and activities, something to spread a little joy to the most fragile lives in every hospital. After Jessie passed away, JoyJars became a staple of the Jessie Rees Foundation. So, too, would Kaitlin.

"When she passed, I was living in Irvine and I wanted to attend her celebration of life that was being held nearby at Saddleback Church," Kaitlin said.

I walked in there and there was not an empty seat in this massive church. They had to stream the service into another room because there were so many people there. I was blown away by how many lives this little girl touched. Erik was a pastor at Saddleback Church at this time and he was leading the service. I don't know how he did that. I was so captured by that entire family. I am a big believer that things happen for a reason. I was supposed to do a photo shoot, but I severely broke my wrist snowboarding, so we had to push it back. But because we had to push it back, the photographer knew about Jessie's story because her celebration of life was so well known in our area. So he thought it would be cool to do part [of the photo shoot] with body paints [spelling out NEGU for "Never Ever Give Up"]. Erik saw those pictures and one thing led to another. I felt like I was waiting for more in my life postswimming, trying to find direction. Erik was sitting down with me trying to help me figure out what that was, all while grieving his daughter and trying to figure out what to do with her foundation. He asked me if I wanted to join them for a hospital visit. One hospital visit has led to more than 160 in over six years. It has been such a huge part of my life.

Kaitlin quickly became the national spokesperson for the Jessie Rees Foundation, something she embraced with pride.

"Jessie has been a huge blessing for me. I am still super involved. It has been awesome to see other swimmers like Nathan Adrian take to it. It is really special. There is nothing greater than doing something for a greater cause, and Jessie and her family have allowed me to do that," Kaitlin said.

When I first started with them, it was the hospital visits and also speaking engagements letting people know what we were doing, and trying to get other athletes involved. Who do I know? Who has a heart? Who has time? Who can get the word out? I was starting with friends and friends of friends. Some really amazing things came together. We did a lot of things like having schools bring in a box of crayons or socks for the JoyJars. We obviously started in the swimming community but have submerged into many professional sports teams. Clay Matthews of the Green Bay Packers has helped out. Olympic gymnast superstar Jordyn Wieber used her platform to spread NEGU, and USA Swimming has embraced NEGU, offering hospital visits to national team members. You can get pulled in a lot of directions to do charity work. Sometimes that is really difficult. It is nice to have a go-to cause, one that I am really involved with. Being one of the USA Swimming legends captains for the 2018 Swim Squads we needed to pick a charity [to compete for]. I didn't have to think twice. I didn't need to research. Boom. I have one.

Erik Rees noticed a connection between Kaitlin and Jessie immediately.

We put together a swim meet where you could do laps or raise money for Jessie. Kaitlin showed up. She was very positive, bright, bubbly, and joyful. She clearly had a compassionate heart. She was the one out of the five that actually spent a lot of time with Jessie. That was a really neat thing to watch. Not every athlete has a compassionate side. That is why I like to call her a compassionate competitor. She has that heart that is huge, but not everybody sees it. At the moment, it made me happy because my daughter was smiling. She had someone who was famous talking with her and playing with her, not looking at her body that was different because of cancer. That meant a lot to me. As time went on, Kaitlin reached out and was wanting to talk to me about how to rebrand her life. I help a lot of people find their purpose. She was so used to being told what to do and where to be for so long. She was trying to figure out self-management and what her new brand was going to be.

It turns out Jessie's brand and Kaitlin's brand would be forever intertwined as Kaitlin went on to become the national spokesperson for the foundation in 2012, whose slogan is "Never Ever Give Up," or "NEGU," for short.

"It became apparent that she really was wanting to use her Olympic network," Erik Rees said.

We invited her on her first hospital visit at the Children's Hospital of Orange County. I think that is when it clicked for Kaitlin. Yes she sat with kids and delivered JoyJars. She won't leave until she feels like it is the right time. We have had other athletes who deliver the JoyJar, take a photo, and stay for a couple minutes. Kaitlin stays for as long as the kids want, or can handle. Her heart even broke more for these courageous kids. She walks into the room caring. She knows her only purpose is to help that child have a better moment and brighten that kid's day. She comes in with the right agenda. She has this incredible, caring heart. It

Kaitlin speaking with Erik Rees at the NEGU Golf Classic. *Pam Musgrave*

creates a lot of excitement when she pulls out her four Olympic medals. We want to deliver JoyJars and encourage them to never ever give up. But for us the huge victory is to give them a few minutes where they are not thinking about cancer. Because they are always thinking about it, and their parents are thinking about it. We have a "courageous medal," and Kaitlin puts that medal on them and uses it as a way to remind them to never ever give up.

Her personality was perfect for this mission of the Jessie Rees Foundation. In fact, everyone who has seen her interactions with these children is completely blown away at how natural and positive she was at all times, something that is difficult, for even a compassionate person to do, in the face of cancer. That includes people heavily involved with the foundation, like Cory Tomlinson.

"She is someone we can always call on to speak on behalf of Jessie's mission. She speaks so eloquently and passionately. We can call on her to speak to a large corporation who needs a keynote speaker, or to an elementary school that is collecting toys by doing a toy drive for us. She always wants to continue Jessie's mission," Cory said.

I take her into children's hospitals all over the country still. The way she steps into the room of a child fighting cancer, no words can truly describe the value she is bringing. For a moment, families can forget about cancer and soak up some time full of joy, smiles, and encouragement. Kaitlin never leaves a room without leaving a legacy of joy. It is people like her, who step out to help in the fight against childhood cancer, that are making a mark on families' lives while they are in the fight of their life. No matter how busy of a season Kaitlin is in, she always has passion for these kids because that is the legacy Jessie left on her. New faces of USA Swimming want to go in and do hospital visits like Kaitlin has. It is because of Kaitlin's advocacy we are able to get those connections with other swimmers like Nathan Adrian and Ella Eastin. Through apparel collaborations, her summer league swim team involvement, or her latest business adventures, Kaitlin always finds a way to use her platform to circle back and help us continue Jessie's mission to encourage every single child fighting cancer to "Never Ever Give Up."

The Jessie Rees Foundation began to grow and continued to make hospital visits to deliver JoyJars to kids throughout the country. Kaitlin went on her first visit in May 2012, and just like meeting Jessie herself, it had a profound impact on her.

"In May 2012, Jessie had just passed, and they wanted to do a hospital visit at the hospital where Jessie had undergone her treatment. There were about four or five of us," Kaitlin said.

I had never done one before, so I didn't really know what to expect. I never really spent that much time in a hospital, either. But, of course, when I was asked, I was honored to be there. I was still getting to know Erik and Stacey. I really didn't know them that well at all. I felt like I had to tread lightly. Here they are going through losing a child, then turning around and doing this a month later.

There was nothing quite like that first step into a hospital room. "I remember being really apprehensive when I went into the first room, but I immediately felt at ease when I got in there. I felt like I had a task at hand, bringing joy and continuing what Jessie had started, and I didn't want to let anybody down, let Jessie down, or let the Rees family down. I simply felt like I was there to bring happiness," she said.

Part of why I was so nervous is because I wasn't sure if I was going to be too sad or emotional going in there. But I actually remember it being exactly the opposite because I really did feel like there was a sense of joy in each room we went into. That was my first experience with how optimistic and positive these kids truly were and are. It always proved true. Every visit it was crazy how many positive vibes I felt from these kids. I felt much more sad [*sic*] for the parents because that wasn't necessarily their vibes. Some of them just looked crushed.

As soon as I was done, it was a rush that I wanted to experience again. I wanted to know if I could do more . . . when was the next visit? I truly enjoyed it and felt shaped for it. I almost felt like my swimming had shaped me for it. I think swimming made me very tough on the exterior, but I know I had a compassionate heart, and I felt like that was perfect for this role. You are there to love on these children.

Kaitlin has a knack for leaving a lasting impression on children. They gravitate toward her, and she leaves them with an exciting, memorable encounter. That goes for any child, not just those she is meeting for the foundation. And you never know when that impression is going to pay even bigger dividends in the future.

Delivering JoyJars for the Jessie Rees Foundation. *Sandeno collection*

Kaitlin representing the strength of the Jessie Rees Foundation. *Dan D'Addona*

"I met Kaitlin when I was seven years old on the pool deck. I was an age group swimmer swimming summer league. She was 17 and had just got back from her first Olympic Games," Cory said.

I vividly remember watching her in the Sydney Games. My dad told me that was her, and I took my picture with her and got her autograph. Like any autograph encounter, I was not expecting her to ever remember me. Thirteen years later, my mom came on staff at the Jessie Rees Foundation when I was in college. My mom busted out that old-time photo and showed Kaitlin. About a year and a half later, I got to remeet her on a professional level. We just hit it off. Our personalities work well together. We hit the road and have been spreading joy all over the country ever since—175 hospital visits in the past few years. There have been so many amazing interactions that I have been able to witness between Kaitlin and kiddos fighting cancer. Together, we have been able to process what it is like in the trenches supporting these kids.

Cory continued,

Part of why Kaitlin is a perfect fit for the Jessie Rees Foundation is the fact that she met Jessie before she moved to heaven. Kaitlin had heard her story, but there was no commitment to what the future was going to hold with the foundation.

She wanted to come meet Jessie and encourage her. The fact that she got to meet Jessie is huge. I can't even say that. I never got to meet her. It is the mission and dream Jessie left us with, to encourage every child fighting cancer to "Never Ever Give Up," that Kaitlin has taken very seriously. Her personality is where it comes from. She has a naturally bright, effervescent, energetic personality that just lights up the room when she comes in. That is what we do. Our job is to treat every kid like a kid at the park; they are kids who deserve to smile and play like kids do at the park. When you have someone as bright as Kaitlin that can immediately get down to their level, can play Legos with five-year-old boys, play princesses with nine-year-old girls. . . . There is a relatability that she provides to these kids. It really enhances the belief that these kids are not identified by their disease; in fact, they get to forget, for a moment, that they even have one. And because of this, she has truly perfected the art of being an advocate in the childhood cancer space.

One of many hospital visits, along with one of many priceless moments. *Sandeno collection*

Every interaction with every child is a little different. Some are overjoyed at the sight of a visitor. Some can barely breathe on their own. Others are barely conscious. Some just want to play and not think about cancer. Kaitlin saw her visits as an opportunity to try to cater to the individual child and help them forget about cancer, even if for only a few minutes, as much as possible.

Some visits stood out more than others. "This was in our California tour. It was 2013, and we were spreading joy from Sacramento to San Diego," Kaitlin said.

It was going to be 14 visits in 21 days. We went to a stop in Northern California actually at a Ronald McDonald House. We were setting up shop there. We got all the JoyJars set up, and we were ready to encourage some kids! There was a little boy with leukemia and who also had Down syndrome. He just took to me. I don't know if it was because we had toys, or because we had the same kind of energy, or whatever, but he was in my arms like the whole time. He was so cuddly and so affectionate. He kept giving me big hugs. His hair was falling out on my black Team NEGU shirt, but it didn't faze me. I was just so taken by his sweetness. It was a surreal experience. That was definitely a special interaction. The foundation was still pretty new at that time, so for Cory and I to experience that together was very special and something we still talk about. My interaction with him and how loving and engaging he was literally shows what the Jessie Rees Foundation is trying to do. We are trying to love on the kids and their families. Each interaction is so different. Some kids you really feel like you bond with. Some kids aren't well enough to really engage. Some kids accept their JoyJars and that's as much engagement as there is. But it's all good regardless. I am just doing what Jessie wanted. She wanted every kid fighting cancer to get a JoyJar.

Cory remembers that visit vividly.

In one of the first three visits we did. We interacted with this little boy who was three and had leukemia and Down syndrome. He was losing his hair. You could tell his parents needed a boost of encouragement. I will never forget this moment. Right when Kaitlin and I walked up to this family, they were the only ones in the lobby. He leaped from his dad's arms right into Kaitlin's arms and was so incredibly happy. The love that little boy was giving her was just incredible. That is one of my favorite stories. I will never forget it.

JoyJars are produced at the Jessie Rees Foundation, and each one is hand stuffed with fun things by foundation volunteers. There is really no set pattern for them and, likewise, no set pattern as to which kid will get which jar, although they are split up into jars for boys and girls, and by age. Oftentimes they bring a smile. Sometimes they look like they were handpicked for the specific child, leaving everyone in the room beaming.

"Sometimes you just get goosebumps as to how things happen," Kaitlin said.

Sometimes it is just a godsend. We have experienced many times when we go in a room and find out the kid really loves a certain sports team or color, then they open their JoyJar and there's that sport in there or their favorite color socks or beanie. It is one of those "we couldn't have planned it better" things. It kind of makes you feel like a superhero when you pull out a JoyJar that is so perfect. . . . "You love football? What do you know, here is a football!" Or, "You love purple, everything in here is purple!" It was put together for this kid on this moment to get this JoyJar.

"At the JoyFactory in California, we have bins of toys separated by age and gender. The toys are collected through toy drives and then placed under the JoyJar stuffing tables," Cory revealed.

We could have yellow, pink, and purple rubber ducks or an assortment of specific sports team items, and at any given time we cannot predict the desires of the child who will be receiving the JoyJar that is being stuffed. It is a volunteer's responsibility to create a jar however they wish. If someone wanted to do a Mickey Mouse theme, the volunteer could do that, but they wouldn't know who it was going to.

One particular visit centered around the color purple, and left a lasting impression. The childhood cancer space is hard. We take pride in putting on armor and going in to bring joy. There was a point in time we patted ourselves on the back for not breaking down, crying in hospital rooms yet.

We are in Miami and we walk into this girl's room. We knew that she was a 10-year-old girl, so we took a JoyJar out of our variety pack, for a 10-year-old girl. When we walked in, everything in her room was purple. Literally everything, her blanket, sheets, pillow, beanie. She was coloring with a purple marker, her dad was even wearing a purple shirt because it was his daughter's favorite. We took a mental note. Then we haven't even opened the JoyJar and the little girl starts crying. We weren't sure what is happening. "I was just so grateful that someone would want to come and see me," she said in tears. Those tears we thought were coming from cancer is not what they were coming from. They were tears of joy. That someone would want to put a smile on her face and spend of moment of their day encouraging her. We totally lost it and collected ourselves. We had to step out for a second. That had never happened before. I have delivered a JoyJar for someone getting a lumbar puncture before. We acted as a distraction during that moment, and boy was the nurse happy we were there to do that. After we collected ourselves, we opened up her JoyJar, and, ultimately, when we opened it up and everything in her JoyJar was purple. It was like we tailored it for her. Purple beanie, purple socks, purple marker, purple notepad, you name it. It just happened to be the JoyJar we pulled out for a 10-year-old girl. The moment of what we call Jessie Magic . . . that was Jessie Magic. We could have never planned that if we tried. We don't know how many kids or which kids we are going to see until we get there because the hospitals can't share that information with us.

We can't think about them as kids with a disease. If the caregiver doesn't tell you what they have, you can't treat them any differently. Based simply out of a lack of understanding, if you know they have brain cancer, you may feel cautious about a simple gesture like putting your hand on their shoulder or a simple high five. The mind-set we have to have is that we are kind of like Santa Claus. We come in and deliver toys to children. We create special moments for these kids. That is how we put our armor on. It's all about the smiles.

Cancer patients come in every shape, size, and age. That keeps Kaitlin and the volunteers on their toes, not knowing if they are going to be visiting with a teenager, a toddler, or any age in between.

There was one memorable visit with an older patient that was particularly emotional for Kaitlin late in 2017.

"We were doing a Pacific Northwest tour. JoyJars are for pediatrics, but some older patients can get forms of pediatric cancer," she said.

We were meeting in a play room and engaging with kids at one of our stops. It was around the holidays. I was spending a lot of time with the children. They were total little love bugs. They were sitting on my lap, and we were playing cards. There was also a young adult in the room with us, but I didn't know she had cancer. I thought she was perhaps a sister or family member. She was older, and she looked fantastic. Then one of the nurses told me she was here for a JoyJar.

I went over and chatted with her. I really was able to bond with her because she was older, and she confided how surreal her experiences were. This was an emotional one for me because she was there for her last day of treatment, and my mom had just finished her treatment a few months prior.

Something few people knew at the time was that Kaitlin's mother, Jill, had just gone into remission after being diagnosed with breast cancer in 2016. It changed the way Kaitlin looked at everything, especially her hospital visits.

"It changed a little bit when she was diagnosed," she declared.

When you are involved with the Jessie Rees Foundation, you know the stats a little more. My mom's obviously wasn't pediatric cancer, but you are just more in tune with cancer in general. It is so sad because you know how much of it exists that without being negative, knowing the stats, and doing the math, someone in your circle personally is probably going to face this terrible disease.

I felt the emotion that I felt when my mom finished her treatment because it was this young lady's last day. I try not to tear up on hospital visits because that is exactly what you are not supposed to do. But this instant, I had to take a moment to collect myself. It was too close to home. And, of course, it happened to be the moment that the local news wanted to talk about the foundation and the visit. It was just too close to home. That was a very personal visit and very relatable.

Kaitlin was alongside Jill during every step of her treatment, something that had an impact on her family that is difficult to put into words. Jill said,

> I will always say that I think her experience with the Jessie Rees Foundation made her strong for it, therefore strong for me. She was educated through something we had never been through. For all my tests, labs, procedures, she already had insights about them.
>
> When I was first diagnosed and after my surgery, she lived with us. She was basically my nurse. It seems surreal. Almost a blur. More mental than physical. My family never let me do one thing alone though. No appointment, treatment, anything. I was never without a member of my family, if not, all of them. The "Fab Five" they would say. They would have to bring in extra chairs to the room so we could all fit. I couldn't of done it without them. The treatment was long. As the doctor told us, "This is going to be a marathon not a sprint." I was fortunate that I did hormone therapy instead of chemotherapy, so in general I mostly felt tired, drained, I didn't feel like myself, but I can't ultimately complain. The hardest part was the radiation every day for 33 days. My life, my schedule revolved around it, and obviously the recovery from my two surgeries was the most physically trying, as I said, I couldn't have done it without the "Fab Five."

Especially Kaitlin. Jill added, "Her pictures in the hospitals, with these children, they were always tough to see, but I remember thinking, 'If these little kids can do it . . .' It inspired me. Basically, if they can do it. I can do it. NEGU!"

It was Kaitlin's calmness that helped the rest of the family, too. "She would always ask doctors for clarification. She was always writing down things in her little notebook. She kept her cool, and I think that calmed the family," her father Tom said.

Knowing what Jill was going through made that particular emotional visit very emotional for Cory as well.

"This past fall, I brought Kaitlin with me on a Pacific Coast tour in Seattle and Portland," Cory said.

Kaitlin and her mom, Jill, were hand in hand for a lot of Jill's treatment, strengthening their already strong bond. *Sandeno collection*

Kaitlin's mom had been diagnosed with breast cancer, and the journey she walked with her mom, going to all the appointments and hearing all of the times anyone said cancer, I knew were tough for Kaitlin. She never thought that she would be hearing those words in her own life. Everything became even more real to Kaitlin. On the tour, we were doing a playroom visit. This older girl walked in. She was 21 and had been diagnosed with a childhood form of cancer, so she was being treated at the children's hospital because of the type of cancer she has. This girl, Kaitlin had a very special interaction with her. She was celebrating her very last day of chemo that day. She was so excited we were there that day. She said to us, "It is crazy that you guys are here today. I actually planned my last chemo today so my favorite caregivers would be here, and I got the bonus of meeting you!" The nurses celebrated with her all day, and as she left the playroom for the final time, we all got to cheer for her. What I remember was what happened as she walked out of the room. Kaitlin came up to me and just started crying. We hugged. Kaitlin said to me, "I remember the day my mom was done with her cancer treatment, and I am reliving those memories." It was such a powerful moment. A year before that, she didn't have that personal touch with cancer. But through her mom's fight, this story was unfolding and it was a very special moment for Kaitlin.

The next day proved how difficult happy endings are to find in a pediatric cancer ward, no matter how much joy can be spread. "The next day, I had a nurse friend who came up to me after coming out of a room," Cory said.

> She told us we need to go in that room. I remember the look she gave me. It was a look of sorrow that through the patient privacy laws, I just knew we had to step up to the task for her. We weren't allowed to actually go in the room because there were droplet precautions, so we had to wait outside. What we found out was the person in that room was the girl we celebrated being cancer free the day before. We have no idea why she was back in the hospital. No one could disclose that information to us. At the end of the day, emotionally, that was one of the hardest things we have dealt with. This is the reality of cancer. She was back in the hospital the next day after celebrating being cancer free, and we couldn't go in and see her. We want to believe it was because her counts were low. We want to believe she is cancer free still. But we were not able to find out. Fighting for these kids doesn't just end when we walk out of the hospital room. We continue to fight for these kids and believe in these kids. Their joy and their desire to fight is why we continue to care until there is a cure.

Just like Kaitlin did for her mother.

Kaitlin wanted to be there for her mother every step of her battle. "My mom was diagnosed, and I kind of put everything on hold and went through everything with her. I am so grateful that I had a schedule that allowed me to do so," she said.

> I was staying at my parents' house a lot, taking her to a majority of her doctor's appointments. We didn't want her to go to anything alone. So when I did my first visit after my mom was diagnosed, everything was a little more raw. I had gone with athletes before, like [baseball players] Nick Punto and Skip Schumaker, strong men who were also fathers. So when they would go in these rooms, it would hit a little bit harder with them. They are like, "That is how old my son is," or, "That is how old my daughter is." I had never experienced that until my mom had cancer. It hits again on a different level. It gets even more personal. My mom is starting to realize that her story can help people, encouraging them to get early checkups.

Not everyone can just drop everything and be there for a parent going through that kind of long-term battle and treatment. Kaitlin lived close by and had the flexibility, with her hands in many jobs but not one completely full-time, to set aside bigger chunks of time, which was a blessing for her mom and her entire family.

"The biggest blessing was that I could be there, especially with how close my family is. We all live in the same vicinity. I had just started coaching my second

Sisters Camlyn and Amy, mother Jill, and Kaitlin have been a huge support system for one another, especially during Jill's cancer treatment. *Sandeno collection*

season with the Lake Forest Dolphins, and their pool is so close to my parents' house, maybe two minutes," she said.

> I would be with my mom all day, go coach, and then come back. My husband was so supportive about me being with her all the time. It was extremely scary when she was first diagnosed. It was a very emotional time. I just remember breaking down in Pete's arms when she was first diagnosed. I don't think I have ever sobbed so hard in my life. I already felt like my family was really close before this, so coming out of it even closer, you wonder how that could even happen. I try to remember how blessed my family is. They called it the lazy cancer, but you still have to go through the treatment for it, which is zapping. My dad took it like a champ. He was on the roller coaster living with it. It wasn't easy that's for sure, but he would never say that.

It wasn't easy for Kaitlin, either. But it made her more vigilant about being there for her family and the Jessie Rees Foundation. Erik Rees has seen the strong bond that connects both parts of Kaitlin's life.

"I have gotten to know her very intimately, and she comes from a great family," Erik Rees said.

They are just genuine, caring people. They set the tone early on in her life that she is super talented, but we are going to be about helping and caring for people. Her sisters are very caring people. The nucleus for Kaitlin is her family unit. There is just love there. That gave her a great foundation to come home to whether she won or lost in swimming. But it helped catapult her heart to helping others. She came to faith later in life, and it is a key component.

A lot has to do with your family origin and your parents. I sense this incredible unity. She still gets together with her family all the time. Kaitlin dropped everything, which was the most beautiful thing. This is what life is all about. Now Kaitlin goes and speaks and does different kinds of things. But she is also opening up a lot of people's minds to the world outside the water and having the opportunity to help. She has even inspired some of her Olympic teammates. I know Rebecca Soni and Jessica Hardy were inspired by her and the children benefited by the Jessie Rees Foundation. I am not saying they wouldn't have done something like this, but they were able to watch her do it and have that influence. She does an outstanding job in front of a camera.

And it all started with that first meeting with Jessie.

"I am proud of my daughter. I am honored that I get to do this," Erik said.

I had no idea that it was going to be something so big. At the time, we were just giving her something to do. JoyJars were her idea, and we wanted to continue it. For me it is not a job, it is more of a life work. I am so stoked that over 200,000 children have gotten JoyJars. We know we are making a difference. That jar opens up a relationship, and we know how important that is. We are honored to be a part of it. I am proud to be Jessie's daddy.

And Kaitlin's friend.

These two strong and inspirational people are forever linked, which, of everything about the foundation, makes Kaitlin the proudest.

"She is in what I call our top five," Erik said.

There are five things that have been instrumental in making us what we are today. Kaitlin Sandeno is one of those. We would not be where we are today without her commitment, desire, and passion. I am thankful that I can call her a good friend, maybe even a great friend. We are better today because of Kaitlin.

And Kaitlin is better today because of Jessie.

2

CALIFORNIA GIRL

Almost two decades before she met Jessie Rees, Kaitlin Sandeno was a young, athletic kid looking for another sport to join.

"You have to be wired a little bit differently to love to go to swim practice. Swimming is hard. I don't even think most swimmers truly enjoy swim practice," Kaitlin said. Kaitlin is wired a little bit differently, but her love of swimming didn't begin right away. "Just try it and we'll get you an ice cream," her mother said. That love of ice cream is in most kids, and it helped open the door to another love—and one of the most successful and versatile careers in the history of swimming.

Kaitlin Sandeno was born March 13, 1983, in Mission Viejo, California, in the heart of Orange County, just a couple of miles from the Pacific Ocean. She is the third daughter of Tom and Jill Sandeno, following older sisters Amy and Camlyn. The family later moved to Lake Forest, a laid-back California city of 77,000, far from the bumper-to-bumper cluster of Los Angeles but also far from a small town. There are plenty of things to do around town, and it is "20 minutes from everywhere," Kaitlin said. It seems like the perfect place for a swimmer to grow up, or any kid for that matter. Kaitlin, like many California kids, loved the water from an early age. "I was a huge water baby," she said. "You couldn't get me out of the bathtub. I was going off the diving board as soon as I was walking. I would jump to my dad, hit the water, and pop up with wide eyes and a big smile, and he would swim me to the side of the pool; then I would proceed to do it all over again."

It wasn't long before Kaitlin was in the pool a little more regularly, following the path of her older sisters. "There was a big age difference between my sisters and I, but I started swimming because they were swimmers. I took a couple of swim lessons," she said. She was so new to the competitive side of the sport that she wasn't sure where the race actually ended. "I started on the Lake Forest Sharks when I was 5 years old. That was our community summer league team. I thought it was a race to get out of the pool at first. I would touch the wall then hop out as quickly as I could and look around to see if I won." What a different sport it would be if that were the case! She quickly learned the race was only in the pool and that she was winning the race to the wall. Sandeno also was extremely energetic and exuberant in everything she did. It began in her neighborhood.

When we were growing up, there were a lot of neighborhood boys my age, and I think that is where I got a lot of my tomboy-ness from. My sisters were so much older than me so it wasn't like I was playing with my sisters the same way most young girls do. Rollerblades, bikes, Nerf football, water fights with the boys, we all grew up on the swim team as well. It was very much the community feeling.

And Kaitlin fit right in, no matter what she was doing. "Love for athletics, any sport, or even boys sports was the biggest thing," her mother Jill said. "She played on a boys soccer team for a tournament and played on a boys water polo

Kaitlin's first Olympics, 1984, in Los Angeles. *Sandeno family*

Kaitlin was ready to swim no matter what age. *Sandeno family*

team before they had girls water polo. She was always enthusiastic to take on anything and everything." But it was the water where she was most comfortable. "She never wanted to get out of the bathtub as a toddler," Jill said.

> She loved being in the water. That was her sassy part of the day: "Kaitlin, time to get out," and she would say, "No!" Tom would take her to the pool, probably 18 months to two years old. She wouldn't even hesitate walking to the end of the diving board and would jump in feet first. She plopped to the bottom and bobbed right up with a huge smile, and Tom would swim her to the side. It made me feel very anxious, but Tom encouraged it.
>
> Since she was a baby, people would stop us and comment what a beautiful child she was and told us she should do beauty contests. We finally gave in around the time she was five. We brought her to a world we had no idea about it. She was so underdone compared to these other children. No hair and makeup. Basic, age-appropriate dress. When she didn't win, Tom grabbed her hand and that was the end of her pageant days. I will never forget how Tom pouted because he just knew he had the cutest daughter. Ha! Her curls. Curls and curls and curls. Our friends called her the "golden girl" way before her swim career. Now, they still do.

The Sandeno family in 1984. *Sandeno family*

Kaitlin's athletic career was something that strengthened her bond with her father. "She was the son that I never had," Tom said with a smirk. "We used to play football in the family room. She would set up an end zone, put on one of my football jerseys, and try to run me over to score. *Monday Night Football* in the family room."

Tom helped ease Kaitlin into the pool—not that she needed much encouragement. "Our pool days stand out," Tom said. "She used to love when I would throw her in the air. Over and over, just launching her. We got her a kiddie pool for the house. She loved being in the water. I remember competitors would say, 'Oh no, that blonde girl is here again.'"

But despite all of that natural ability and desire, something that threatened her athletic ability was her asthma, something she didn't know she had until she got a little older. "When I was younger, I played a lot of sports. After running in soccer games, I would constantly be coughing," said Kaitlin.

For the longest time, my parents thought it was because I was working so hard out there. Then the common cold would turn into bronchitis quickly. I would get that and then have this lingering cough. We finally went to the doctor for my reoccurring bronchitis. He threw out the word "asthma," and I immediately thought asthma meant no sports. I started crying. I was heartbroken. There wasn't a lot of education about asthma and sports at the time. But then he explained about inhalers and everything. My parents felt bad that they didn't put two and two together sooner. For me my symptoms were every cold turned to bronchitis or a sinus infection. I just got sick a lot. I feel like I can't catch my breath when I'm pushing myself hard. I yawn a lot because when I yawn I feel like I get a bigger breath. It comes in waves though; it's not a daily feeling.

It wasn't a sports-induced asthma, which a lot of these cases are. Once I went to see *Phantom of the Opera* with my mom and sisters, and when the fog came in for the scene, I had a full-on asthma attack. I had to leave the theater because I couldn't breathe. I describe it like trying to breathe through one of those thin coffee straws. I had to go through all the paperwork for drug testing to prove that you have asthma. It wasn't until my stress fracture [in college] that I actually got my asthma under control. I coughed all the time, and it wasn't allowing my stress fracture to heal, it was pulling it apart. That is when I saw a specialist and got some medication that started working. I always wonder what it would have been like to swim without it. I thought it meant no sports when I was younger, which obviously wasn't the case, but it definitely made it challenging. I had to leave a swim meet in Santa Clara because of an asthma attack. [Coach] Mark Schubert just sent me home. I had one in China at a big meet. And also at the 2000 Olympic training camp and a handful while training indoors while I was in Michigan. They always come at not ideal times. I like to share that I competed with asthma during my speaking engagements because I think it can encourage other kids that face the same issue. It sucks, but it's not a deal breaker.

For Kaitlin, they came at soccer games, on the pool deck, and just about everywhere in between. But she never let it affect her athletic ability or work ethic, which she carried with her in every activity of her life.

The vast array of activities kept Sandeno constantly on the move as she wove her way through a plethora of sports and activities. "Lake Forest is a smaller town, but that gave me a great feel of community support. I love Orange County, and it is such a mecca for athletics and specifically for swimming. But I wouldn't say swimming was my first love—definitely soccer was," she said.

There were definitely some days where I didn't want to swim. I was really good at soccer. I loved the sport. I was pretty athletic. Some swimmers aren't necessarily good at land sports, but I was. I did water polo before there was a girls' team, so I was on a guys' team. I was like a tomboy with a bow in my hair, because I was definitely girly, too. My mom tried to find me a year-round swim club that would let me play soccer, too. At about 10, I knew I wasn't going to swim full time at that point. I wanted to keep playing soccer. My mom called around and

Kaitlin focusing at an all-star soccer game in February 1993. *Sandeno family*

met coaches to find the best fit for me at that age. We ended up signing up with the Nellie Gail Dolphins, and I never left [our team ended up merging a few years later]. People ask why I didn't change to a big Southern California powerhouse team once I stopped soccer. There was nothing wrong with the situation. I was happy there. I liked the small team, and I loved my coaches, and I was swimming fast, so why leave?

Swimming paid immediate dividends for Sandeno in school, whether she realized it at a young age or not. "I was good in school. I wasn't Einstein, but I behaved, got my work done, and got strong grades," she related. "I had good time management skills. There wasn't a lot of time to dilly-dally. I was a huge sleeper. The hardest part for me was the morning workouts."

As with any athlete who had to deal with odd scheduling, her family was instrumental. "[My role is] total support," her mother Jill said in a USA Swimming Mother's Day interview in 2000.

Just be there when she needs me. Kaitlin still thinks there's 48 hours in the day. She does so much with school and so much with swimming. You put the two together and it's quite a combination, but she's really good with her time management and her priorities. Whatever she doesn't have time for, I try to help her with. I try to make her life as stress-free as it can be, under the circumstances.

But work ethic was never something Sandeno lacked. She had a tremendous role model in that department living under the same roof. "Some of my athletic genes definitely come from my dad," she said.

My dad is the epitome of a hard worker. He is the best. Just thinking about how hard he has worked for us makes me tear up. I remember he would work three jobs so my mom wouldn't have to work so she could take us to everything. He could fix your house, your roof, your deck, and everyone wanted him to do that. Everyone loves my dad. He has a really nice way about himself. He is kind of quiet and doesn't have to run the show but has a strong presence. He couldn't come to everything because of work, but he would try his best. He would take me to morning swim practices. Poor guy, I was the worst in the morning. I hardly

Kaitlin and her dad danced to the song "Just Fishing" at her wedding. And here they are doing just that in Mammoth Lakes, California. *Sandeno family*

said a word. I remember most just listening to country music with him on the way to the pool not saying a word. He didn't try to pry anything out of me, just let me sit there as a grumpy morning person. He is how I know what hard work is and how to push through pain. I've seen him push through back, shoulder, and knee injuries without complaining. He is a total badass, but a subtle badass.

Tom is a perfect complement to Sandeno's mother, Jill. "My mom is my best friend. I feel like I never had that awkward phase with my mom where everything she does annoys or embarrasses you," Kaitlin reflected.

I have never met anyone so patient and so loving. I don't get patience from her. That is one of my weaknesses. My mom was a figure skater, and she was my soccer coach growing up. She always said, no matter what, "Be a nice girl." She gets very emotionally proud if someone tells her she has nice daughters . . . much prouder than someone saying, "Kaitlin's a great swimmer." My parents gave me constant, constant support and unconditional love. I was never afraid to fail in the

Jill teaching Kaitlin how to ice skate in Lake Arrowhead, California. *Sandeno family*

pool because I wasn't afraid of letting my parents down because of a bad swim. I knew that didn't matter to them. That unconditional love and support made me not afraid to succeed or fail. I knew I was loved no matter what place I finished.

That support was also there from her older sisters, even if it came in different forms. "I would want to hang out with them and have them include me. Camlyn was a cheerleader and super popular, and I was her shadow when I could be," Kaitlin said. Camlyn had a constant companion at her heels. "When I got into cheerleading, she wanted to do my cheer clinics, and she was right behind me doing the cheers. When she really got into competitive swimming, it definitely brought our family close because we understood it." It was a way that sisters so far apart in age could share a bond. "Cam is 11 years older. She came to everything," Kaitlin added. "For a sister who is that much older than you and had her own life, she came to my photo shoots . . . everything." Amy is the oldest, 13 years older than Kaitlin. "When she was born, I was 13, and I was so excited. I wanted to feed her at night. Then I turned 16, and my attention went elsewhere. Our bond came later. I was always the proud, supportive big sister, and I always felt a little on the outside because I was older and married and having kids," Amy said. It was the start of a somewhat maternal bond as the older sister.

Sister love. Kaitlin, Amy, and Camlyn. *Sandeno family*

Said Kaitlin, "Growing up she was perhaps more like a mother figure because she was already 13 when I was born. I don't remember my childhood as much with her because of the age difference. But we have a huge bond now as adults."

In fact, the entire family seems to get closer by the day. Everyone lives, like Kaitlin said, 20 minutes away, and that makes for a lot of interaction. "We spend a lot of our time together. They are my everything. We still do family vacations, birthdays, all the holidays, and any excuse to get together," Kaitlin revealed.

But before the family was constantly together, it was constantly in motion. As Amy and Camlyn were finishing high school and doing their own things, Kaitlin was becoming a swimmer.

"I started coaching Kaitlin when she was 8," Renee Riggs said.

I remember her being sweet and very energetic. She has always had more energy than the average person. At that time, she was doing multiple sports and always playing soccer. That went on for a good number of years. She came to as many practices as she could, but she really was a part-time swimmer those first couple of years. She was tiny. She was a thin child. You didn't think of her as someone who would have that athletic destiny. One of the things that led to her success is even at a young age, she wasn't intimidated by anybody. She wasn't fazed by who was in the lane next to her. I don't think she ever got up on the blocks and didn't think

Kaitlin holding up her ribbons after a swim meet. *Sandeno family*

she could win this—but not in a cocky way. . . . She never left a swim practice where she didn't say thank you. I think in the span of 30-plus years, I only had a handful that said thank you each and every day. She was the first.

There was a pretty solid gap between her sisters and her. But she was going to all kinds of events watching her sisters compete. The sooner she could get out there the better. I recently saw a video of when she was five years old and she was behind the blocks stretching in a routine that looked like a kid much older than she was. She was a good 9–10 swimmer. She was a good 11–12 swimmer. It was between 12–13 when she started picking up cuts. She was a breaststroker first. Her first juniors cut was in the 200 breaststroke.

In addition to thinking winning the race meant being the first to get out of the pool, Kaitlin's earliest swim memories include learning the different strokes and experiencing different pools—there were plenty—all within 20 minutes.

"I remember when I first started swimming the breaststroke I would look around while racing. I remember the Janet Evans swim facility when I started racing club," she said. "I remember getting my first Olympic trials cut in the 200 breast. My team was super supportive. I got a junior national cut in the 400 IM, and I had no idea until a timer told me."

But once she got a junior nationals cut, a nationals cut followed, and Olympic trials cuts came after that. The qualifying swims began to fall like dominoes. Sandeno ascended quickly as a youth swimmer, and, in 1996, she got to see what Olympic swimming was all about and what those qualifying times could lead to in the future. The Atlanta Olympic Games featured 14-year-old Amanda Beard, who was born in Newport Beach and grew up in Irvine, the next city northwest of Lake Forest. "Amanda Beard grew up in this area, so her first Olympics was the first one I remember watching. She was 14. That is insane," Kaitlin declared. "I knew her and swam against her. She was a lot faster than me. We were swimming some breaststrokes together. But when I started getting to her level it was in the fly and the IM for me."

That experience of watching Beard at the Olympics and on late-night talk shows was eye-opening. Kaitlin continued,

She was 14, and I was 12 or 13. I knew she was from our area, and that is when I started swimming club. I thought it was so surreal. She was so young, and all the coverage she got with her iconic teddy bear. I was blown away that you could be that good at that age. And when someone is from your area, it makes them more relatable. Then you go to meets and she would be there, and then we were swimming together and against each other. There was always that one high school meet where I had to swim against Amanda, and everyone would be watching

Kaitlin on starting blocks at a summer league swim meet in July 1990. *Sandeno family*

every year. She would just whoop me in the breaststroke. It made our area of high school swimming very exciting. I think that made me a better swimmer. We just have great memories together.

Meanwhile, while watching the Olympics, Kaitlin continued to get faster. She was such a natural athlete that success followed her just about everywhere she went. "The joke about Kaitlin is everything she touches turns to gold," Camlyn said. "She always ran and got first place. In soccer, she was getting goals. In swimming, she was winning. I remember people in the stands asking if I thought she was going to make the Olympics. And she was eight years old."

It was in the pool that Kaitlin began to meet people she has been close to her entire adult life. Teammates like Amy Walloch. "We did not go to the same elementary school," Amy said,

> but we became friends through swim practice. She always likes to claim that my house is the first house that she spent the night in when she was a kid. We would have sleepovers and hang out a lot growing up. Until I was about seven, I lived there and swam with the Sharks. Then I became a competitor against her for the next couple years. I was then on the Dolphins and she was on the Sharks. She was kind of shy actually. I have always been very loud and she is very much like that now, but she was kind of quiet when we were young. Maybe in junior high she started blossoming and her personality started coming out. I don't know how she was in school, but that was the one thing that stuck with me. She was so shy. Even though she was so small, she was just so fast. She was always one of the top swimmers in our age group even from a very young age.

Her speed never affected her personality. Out-of-pool drama was something Kaitlin was always able to avoid—no simple task in a pool full of adolescent girls. "She was someone I always looked up to," said teammate Bree Deters.

> She always had really good balance and played soccer and did other things, too. She is just such a nice person. I don't think she ever went through that middle school phase where everyone is mean to each other. It happens in those tween years. Junior high she definitely started getting more involved. She was becoming one of the more popular girls.

But just like her speed never affected her personality, neither did her social status. Kaitlin remained the down-to-earth, friendly-to-everyone person she had always been. "I have known Kaitlin for a really long time. She is a couple years older than me. I was about seven. We were on the same small swim club," Bree Deters said. "Our families were really close growing up. In addition to all the

Kaitlin (right) with Bree Deters. It is easy to see why people thought they were sisters. *Sandeno family*

soccer games we had in our family, we went to Kaitlin's games, too. Our families would go to this local pizza joint on Friday nights. There were a lot of times with her around the pool deck."

In fact, Kaitlin and Bree were together so much, they were often mistaken for sisters. Of course, it didn't hurt that they looked pretty similar. "When we were younger, we used to joke about looking like sisters. They always asked if we were sisters, and we used to giggle like 10-year-olds do," Bree said.

> We thought it was really funny. Even after she started making it big, making the Olympic team, she was such a good sport about it because people would come up to me and ask me for my autograph, thinking I was her. Sometimes I would tell them I wasn't her, sometimes I would be like, "Yeah, I'm Kaitlin," and sign her name on things. She would just get completely bombarded with people. But when we were on our small club team with cap and goggles, and swimming similar events, it was really easy for people to confuse us.

Kaitlin had that ability to remain in the moment no matter what she was doing, whether that be pretending to be sisters with a friend, concentrating on her schoolwork, or preparing for a big race. Sometimes the compartmentalization allowed her to switch her focus from one thing to another instantly. "I remember working hard, but every set we would race to the wall so we could gossip and giggle for a minute. It used to drive our coach crazy. We used to have so much fun with each other and the other girls on the team. It was social hour, but we also worked hard," Deters said.

The hard work grew as Kaitlin started to grow—even with major changes that crept up on her throughout her middle and high school years.

It started with a change in her club in 1995. The Nellie Gail Dolphins merged with another team as Kaitlin's coach, Renee, married Vic Riggs, who was the coach of the other small club. The relationship blossomed quickly and led to quite a bit of success for the swimmers. But Renee was worried the club would split and end up dissolving.

"I remember thinking that I was going to lose every person on that team. Kaitlin stayed, and most of the kids stayed," she said.

My team and my husband's team trained together, and we each had some kids who were really good. Plus my husband's team had a 50-meter pool in El Toro. We joke that I just needed his pool. That summer we started doing practices together. I remember us watching the group, and he saw it then in Kaitlin and I think she was 12. We had some really good kids, some that went to Olympic trials and swam NCAA Division I, but I remember him telling me that he thought Kaitlin was the one to keep an eye on.

It didn't happen right away, though. But when it did, it was an awakening for Vic and Renee. "Renee and I met in early 1995," Vic said.

May is when we went on our first date. By that summer, we decided to get married and merge our programs. In August, right before I went on vacation, we made a proposal to inform them that we wanted to combine programs, the Nellie Gail Saddleback Valley Gators. That fall of 1995 is when I first met Kaitlin. She was heavily involved in soccer and swimming. Tiny kid. No muscle. A little 13-year-old girl that was good at swimming. Renee was getting to know my kids, and I was trying to get to know hers. Kaitlin was the youngest swimmer in the senior group by far.

But there was a moment where Vic could see the path to greatness.

I would have to say when we did one of our test sets once a month. One of them was 3,000 for time. It was the first or second practice that first year. She kept looking over at the other swimmers. It was bugging me because she kept looking and her turns weren't crisp, but I figured out she was gauging where she was to beat the other swimmer. That is when I realized she had no fear of other swimmers. That was the first time I was like, "Wow this kid could be something special."

Sandeno attended El Toro High School and was faster than some of the boys, despite her small stature at the time. "I was tiny," Kaitlin said. "We look at pictures and I think I am in seventh grade and my mom would be like, 'No you were in high school there.'"

Kaitlin was, in fact, a late bloomer, and adolescence was something Renee watched transform Kaitlin. "She went through puberty—late—and her body changed. When her body changed, her strengths changed. That is one of the reasons I think pushing kids that haven't gone through it in one direction is kind of crazy," Renee said.

While Kaitlin was swimming well in her revamped club, she also was unleashed in high school pools for the first time. It made for even more time in the pool. While this could be a frustrating and exhausting situation for Kaitlin and her parents, the coaches got together and came up with a plan so she was not overworked and participated enough in both places.

"El Toro High School had a really strong water polo team at the time, but not as strong in swimming. The water polo players were kind of forced to swim. These are the boys I grew up with, so it made it very fun and entertaining," Kaitlin related.

My club team trained at my high school, so it was my home away from home. It was so convenient because it was right down the road. I was allowed to do the high school swim practice, but if I did, I had to stay for my club practice. Since I didn't want to swim for five hours, I didn't practice with my high school often. My coaches worked out deals about when I would be where. Which meets I could race at, and if I trained with them it needed to be with the guys team.

That is a theme that would continue into her professional career.

She was also versatile enough. In fact, she would go on to become one of the most versatile athletes in the history of women's swimming. It started early with a broad skill set and a philosophy at her club that was conducive to versatility.

"She really doesn't have a weak stroke, so the IM seemed like the logical thing to always do. Our philosophy has always been freestyle a couple days a week, strokes a couple days a week, and IM a couple days a week. It exposes them to everything, helps them not get injured," Renee Riggs said.

Maybe you find an event you didn't realize you would be good at. She was early high school when it was apparent she was pretty good. We went to a summer meet and she had not done the 200 fly before and we thought she should try it. I believe she made a national cut in it the first time she swam it. Obviously that became one of her best events, but she never trained a lot of fly—at least not at that point. She swam it, she actually swam a 1,650-yard fly once. She wanted to try it. It was the 1,650 freestyle, and she wanted to do it fly, so we let her. We were wary about it because you worry about kids' shoulders, but she came out of it okay.

That sounds like a nightmare to most people, even most butterfliers, but it was something Kaitlin wanted to do to make her stroke more rhythmic. "It was a smaller meet. It was only the mile on the first night. I was trying to get out of Saturday morning workouts," she said.

I was like, "Since we are racing tonight, we don't have to come in the morning right?" He [Vic] was like, "If you do the mile all butterfly and get the junior national cut, you don't have to come to morning practice.'" I told my mom. She was like, "You are not going to do that, are you?'" I said no, then thought about it some more. I went back and forth.

I was behind the blocks, and I realized I could always start it and switch since it was a freestyle race. It was short course. I had good underwaters. I remember taking my mark, and I was like, "I am going to do it!" I remember feeling decent. I think I still won or got second but just missed the junior cut. My mom couldn't believe I did it. Afterward, I got a terrible head rush. Because I did so much under water, my sinuses were shot. I felt sick afterward. I still had to go to practice, but Vic let me go after the warm-up set. I think it was the challenge.

Competitiveness, backed by her natural ability, work ethic, and mental strength, is something that separated Kaitlin from other swimmers. Renee Riggs saw that ability and her ability to have balance. "I think it was a combination of things. Number one, she is physically gifted. She is not big, but she is very strong. Her strength-to-body-weight ratio has always been really good," Renee said. "She has good strokes and a great feel for the water. What went on under the surface was always a powerful force for her. She had great catch and was very strong in all of her strokes."

But that is only half of the puzzle. "She trained harder than any athlete I have ever had," Renee continued.

She frequently trained with the boys. Our senior group had maybe 25 kids, and there were two or three that were going to junior nationals. It is not like she had some crazy training team, but there were a couple boys who were good, and she

Kaitlin graduating from eighth grade. *Sandeno family*

trained with them. We did a lot of yards, but probably 7,500 per practice in the afternoon and 4,500 in the morning. She was putting in mileage.

While she was using that natural ability and working hard, there was a third element that is difficult to cultivate in an athlete unless it is already there. "I cannot overstate the importance of her mental strength. She was never intimidated. She never shied away from a race. She always felt she had an opportunity to win it," Renee said. "The flip side of that is she never made things the biggest deal. Winning the race was not the focus, it was about doing your own best. You can't control what the person in the next lane is doing anyway. She was good at compartmentalizing that."

She was able to compartmentalize more than just her work in the water. Swimming can dominate anyone's calendar, but unlike most elite swimmers, Sandeno continued to be involved in other activities. She was the class president from sixth grade until her junior year and school vice president her senior year.

Being involved made school more fun. I legitimately enjoyed planning our pep rallies and other school activities. I loved planning prom. My mom encouraged student council in grade school, and I loved it ever since. I kind of ended up running unopposed for a few years for our class president because I just kept doing it until my senior year. I was going to miss the beginning of the school year because of the Olympics so I ran for school vice president instead. There were perks that came with it. I like the leadership role. I enjoy leading—definitely more of a leader than a follower. I was definitely flattered that my classmates wanted me—or at least didn't think they could beat me.

She added, with a smirk, "I guess there is some competitiveness there, too."

That competitiveness began to grow in the water as Kaitlin continued to gain speed. She was always ahead of the majority of girls her age until it reached a point where she was starting to compete at a national level in 1998.

I was good when I was five to 10 years old, then I would say I was in the middle of the pack until I got a little bit taller and bigger at 13. That's when I stopped playing soccer. I still miss soccer. I was really torn because I legitimately loved that sport, and I was pretty good, too. I had coaches that believed in my swimming career so much. It became unfair to the soccer team because I wasn't always there. I am so glad I played. I actually played on a coed team right before I got married. That was a blast. My brother-in-law Steve was on the team as well. My family would come watch our games on Friday nights. It was awesome! At 14, I was starting to go to juniors and win. PanAms [1999 Pan American Games] was when I was 16, and that's where I truly started to realize my potential. Got some height, put some weight and muscle on, and just did what I was told and wham-bam!

It felt that fast for the people around her, too. "She was different. What stood out was when she was 13, she got her junior nationals cut in the breaststroke. She was this teeny tiny little kid and got to go to this really big meet," Bree Deters said.

Pretty quickly after her first junior meet, she then qualified for nationals. It seemed like she blew up in a six-month period. It still wasn't like I was thinking she was going to make the Olympic team. It wasn't until the year before Olympic trials that I thought she could really do this. A lot of it is because of her personality. Knowing her outside of the pool, she is so down to earth.

Kaitlin competed at the USA national championships and finished sixth in the 800 freestyle, touching the wall in 8:41.60, despite 100-degree temperatures at the Clovis Olympic Swim Complex on August 11, 1998. Just 15, her sixth-place finish put her on the USA national team for the first time in 1999, and she competed at the Pan American Games in Winnipeg, Manitoba, Canada. Diana Munz, then 16, who would go on to be her Olympic teammate and roommate in 2000 and 2004, won the race in 8:31.74.

"It feels great," Kaitlin told the *Orange County Register.* "I've just trained really hard this summer. I just put it all together." After turning 16, she finished second in the 800 at the USA national championships on March 28, 1999, at East Meadow, New York. Two days later, she won the 400 IM in 4:43.37—her first national championship—a full seven seconds faster than she had ever swum the race. "When I touched the wall, I thought, 'Oh my gosh' . . . and I wanted to call my mom really bad," Sandeno told the *Orange County Register.* "I called her. She started crying, and then I started crying."

As odd as it was when she was winning national championships, Sandeno then returned to compete for El Toro High School. She won Southern Sectional titles. She won the 200 IM in a California Division I record time of 2:00.19. She also won the 500 freestyle in 4:43.99. "My work is paying off," she told the *Register.*

Those performances at ages 15 and 16 put Sandeno on the map as a future Olympic contender, although it was rarely discussed at that point. "Her coaches never talked about the Olympics," her mom said. But those conversations began to creep into Sandeno's life in 1999. They were unavoidable, especially when she was picked for a National Select camp.

> The first time I got picked for an Olympic select camp in Colorado, I was in tears. I felt like I was the slowest person there. I missed home. But ESPN highlighted it, and I was picked as someone they followed around. I wanted to go home, but then it was like, "Oh I am on TV!" We were in a classroom setting, and they asked everybody who wanted to go to the Olympics and everybody raised their hand except for me. I was like, I play soccer! So perhaps the World Cup! I was never one of those people who was set on going to the Olympics. It wasn't until I went to Winnipeg [for the PanAm Games] and won a couple of events that I knew I had a chance to be an Olympian.

But at that camp in Colorado, Kaitlin crossed paths with someone who would be an incredible opponent and Olympic teammate throughout the years—Natalie Coughlin. While Kaitlin remembers not knowing what she wanted out of her future and being nervous because of the news crews there, it didn't show. Coughlin was immediately impressed with Kaitlin's poise in front of the cameras at such a young age—something she still marvels at when she is on a set with Kaitlin. Said Coughlin,

> I first got to know Kaitlin at a camp at the Olympic center. We had cameras following us around. We were giving them a tour, and Kaitlin totally took charge and was super energetic. She was perfect at it even then. That is the one thing that

I really remember from that camp, just hanging out with her and [another girl]. At that point, I definitely wanted to make the Olympics, but I didn't really know what that path and process was like.

They were both about to find out.

Just 16 years old, Sandeno wasn't sure what to expect out of the PanAm Games, and neither were her coaches. It turned out Winnipeg was the place where Sandeno would explode onto the international swimming scene. She won the 400-meter freestyle and 800 freestyle, breaking Pan American records in both events. She won the 400 freestyle in 4:10.74, the first victory for the U.S. women in Winnipeg, in the sixth event of the meet.

"On the last 25 meters, I was thinking about our team the whole time," Sandeno said in the postrace interview. "Everyone was saying we had to get the first girls gold medal. And I was thinking, 'C'mon guys, I am going to do it for you.' It was awesome." That is when Kaitlin began to look at things from a different perspective. "I was like, 'Oh, maybe I could go to the Olympics'—and next year was the Olympics." She was finally believing what many were starting to see.

It was almost an awakening at Winnipeg, like, "Oh yeah, I am pretty good." Everybody else talked about it except for my coaches and me. It was obviously in the back of our heads, but it wasn't necessarily what I was training for. I think I had one meeting about it with my coaches. They told me they thought I had a chance at making the Olympic team and asked if that was something I wanted to train for. I said yes, and they were like, okay we will discuss with your parents, and that was it really. We didn't really talk about it again but just got to work in and out of the pool.

That was important from her coaches' perspective as well. Vic and Renee realized what made Kaitlin successful and didn't want to disturb any of that by talking about the Olympics too much. Said Renee,

She just had fun with that. She had her most success when she was really enjoying the swimming. The times when I saw her struggle was when things had become too serious. In 1999, she had come back from the Pan American Games. We sat down in the bleachers and asked her if she wanted to try to make the Olympic team. So, we said, let's talk about it right now because after this, we are never going to talk about it again. We never discussed making the team. We discussed swimming as fast as we could. That was extremely important. Swimming fast is fun, and she wanted to have fun.

But the dream had now become a realistic goal, and all eyes were on this teen phenom who could swim a variety of events, which was rarely seen—until now.

3

A KID DOWN UNDER

Everywhere Kaitlin looked, eyes were on her. There weren't many teenagers with a strong chance at making the Olympic team, especially in 2000. But as the 2000 Olympic trials approached, there were two teenagers with big dreams—and the talent to make those dreams a reality. One was 16-year-old Michael Phelps, still yet to burst onto the scene. The other was a 17-year-old with long, curly, blonde locks. Unlike Phelps, who was seen as the future, not yet the present, Kaitlin Sandeno's performance for Team USA in Winnipeg put her on the map as an Olympic contender. It opened the eyes of everyone around her, even those closest to her.

"I thought she would do well [at the PanAms], hoping she would finish in the top eight. I had no idea she would get to first and a record. But then she's always full of surprises. My hopes for her at any meet are just that she's healthy and can swim the best that she's trained for," her mother Jill said in a USA Swimming Mother's Day interview.

With everything that's going on, it's almost surreal. When you step back and look at what's been happening over the last year, it's kind of like, "Wow." She amazes us every time we watch her swim and say, "That's our daughter." And it's a strange feeling sometimes. We just want her to enjoy the sport and feel good about what she's accomplished. With all the hype going into the Olympic trials, I can't tell you how many times a day people ask if she is going to the Olympics. I just tell them she still has to go to the trials and if she stays healthy she has a good chance. We are so very proud and excited about all that she has accomplished in her lifetime.

And it was just beginning.

"She just soaked everything up that we presented to her. Kaitlin would have in some capacity been an Olympian with any coach. For us, she had total trust in what we were doing and just soaked it up," Vic Riggs said.

Even to the days when I was on the deck at USC with Coach Schubert, you only had to tell her once and it was changed. She was oblivious to how good she really was. There were times we would be watching her swim, one meet around 1998, and the girl had never swum a 200 fly long course. It was the first meet of the summer, and we made the kids swim every event [throughout the season]. She swam the 200 fly and made the U.S. national cut. We are watching her swim this 200 fly, and we were like maybe we had to start doing this event, too. She came up to us afterward and just had no idea at what she had just done. At that point, she just got in and swam. A lot of that led to what happened to her in 2000. We managed to adjust the training for her and a few others at that point. We sat down in the fall for goal meetings. We made an agreement that we weren't really going to talk about making the Olympic team, we were just going to do what we needed to do training-wise.

A month or two out, we hadn't started to taper for trials, and she had a little bit of a meltdown after a practice. We told her we were glad that meltdown was happening because we knew how she was feeling and how much she was stressed out with everything. After that, we got the old Kaitlin back.

First, she had to get to the trials, which turned out to be as difficult to get to physically as it was to qualify. There was a huge storm that canceled a lot of flights. Many swimmers had to rent cars and drive the rest of the way to Indianapolis for the trials, putting a severe dent in the plans and last-minute training for a large group of athletes.

"We were supposed to fly to Indianapolis, and Kaitlin ended up riding with another team because everyone was scrambling," Renee said. "Then Vic and our [infant daughter] Abigail and I were in a car together. It was terrifying. Thunder and lightning everywhere. No visibility. But we all got there. Fortunately, we went out there ahead of time."

"It was crazy just getting to trials," Kaitlin remembered. "Going to trials, there was a storm. We got stuck with other teams and had to drive in pouring rain and thunder."

Coming into the trials at Indianapolis, Sandeno had a flood of thoughts and emotions racing through her brain. She was still in high school, yet was one of the best swimmers in the world. She could prove herself to her country at the trials—as long as she didn't let the situation overwhelm her.

"I didn't sleep very much. It was hard to sleep because I was so excited," Sandeno said.

It was the first time I felt like people were staring. I got the sense that the swimming community predicted me on that team before I had even raced. It was like everyone knew except me. That is not to say I wasn't confident. I was. I remember feeling great, but making the Olympic team wasn't something that I had stressed over. I was there to race, my absolute favorite thing about swimming. I get to step up on those blocks and let it rip. And if I happen to place first or second, so be it. The meet was smaller in the sense that not as many swimmers qualified for trials, so it was kind of more intimate. But you could feel the intensity on the deck, like no other meet I had been to. I remember blasting the Vega Boys on the way to the pool. I think that is how I calmed my nerves, just dancing going to the pool. Trying to pretend like this wasn't the biggest meet of my swimming career yet. We were all pretending like we weren't nervous. I know I have mechanisms. Instead of crying I laugh, or in this case, I kept dancing.

Kaitlin didn't have to dance around for long. The 400-meter individual medley was on the first day of the trials, and it was her coaches, Vic and Renee Riggs, who had to dance around to get ready.

"We were getting ready to watch her swim the finals of the 400 IM at the Olympic trials. Teri McKeever took Abigail for me so I could actually watch her race," Renee said. "A coaching friend came up to us and said that we must be the most nervous people on the deck right now. We were like, 'Why?' And he said because if anyone was poised to make the team it was Kaitlin. It floored us because we weren't even there yet."

But they were "there," just maybe in denial. They had prepared for the year, including a trip to the Olympics, something that was not a given and not easy for a young family to put together. There were monetary issues, timing issues, and child-care issues. But Vic and Renee knew they couldn't pass it up. "In February of that year, Vic said we needed to go to the Olympics," Renee said. "We believed [Kaitlin] could make the team, but that is early to buy those tickets and spend that money, especially if she didn't make it. We got our tickets for $799 round trip. By the time the Olympics came around it was $1,700."

"I told Renee that going to the Olympics was on my bucket list," Vic said. "We started saving money as soon as we got married. I found an unbelievable fare. We kind of told Kaitlin that we had ours. . . . It showed our belief in her."

Kaitlin was about to get there. As she dove in for her first final, Sandeno built a lead. "I felt strong and in control for the first half of the race," she said.

Once I got to the breaststroke, I felt totally off. This was the generation of the new full-leg suits. Being on a small team and relatively new to the big scene made it hard to get our hands on the new tech suit ["sharkskin"] to practice in much

Kaitlin, along with coaches Vic and Renee Riggs, as well as their daughter, Abigail, leading up to the Sydney Olympics. *Sandeno collection*

beforehand. I did not like how the suit felt on my legs for breaststroke. I'm mid-race and I am so annoyed to be in this suit. I want to rip the legs off it. I can feel Maddy Crippen gaining on me. "Please just get me to the freestyle!" Luckily, I kept my lead, although much smaller, after breaststroke, and I knew I was home free with my freestyle leg.

Despite her suit issues during the race, Sandeno was able to hold off the entire field. Her time of 4:40.91 gave her a national championship and punched the first U.S. ticket to Sydney.

"I was an emotional mess afterward. I just wanted to find my parents," she said.

I couldn't believe I made the team. Then you have to do processing. We were out on the balcony and were asked a few questions. I said, "I am going to kick butt for

Team USA." It was chaotic. And then seeing my name being painted on the wall first gave me the goosebumps. Pinch me, is this really happening? Now I realize the "wow factor" of making the team at age 17.

It was almost an out-of-body experience for Vic and Renee as well.

"She really was in control of the race in the 400 IM the entire time. She never went out too hard in her 100 fly in design. Our strategy is to always make sure you have enough on the back half," Renee said.

Our basic plan is to work the back half after being smooth on the front half. You have to swim it like you train it. Her goal was to have a solid first 400 and race the back half. We knew after the breaststroke she was good because she had never split the breaststroke like that. There is a picture of her pointing at us, and we had tears in our eyes. I remember her up there getting her award, looking up at the American flag, and really realizing what she accomplished. It was overwhelming.

"About six to eight months before trials, we had to change our plan for the 400 IM because of the breaststroke," Vic revealed.

Her butterfly and backstroke were so good, we wanted her to just go . . . then she would be so far ahead of the others that she could have a little bit of a weaker breaststroke and still be okay. They had changed the format to having the trials just a little bit before the Olympics. With the 400 IM being the first event. She split at 2:11 or 2:12 and was probably four body lengths ahead, and I said, "Holy cow! I think it is going to happen." The last 20 meters we were just going crazy. That was really cool to see her be the first kid on the team.

She had made the team, but there was still a week of swimming to go.

After the initial shock of making the team subsided, Sandeno's performance in the 400 IM jump-started a fantastic week of swimming. After making the Olympic team on the first night, the momentum continued from there.

"As the meet went on, there were people telling us she didn't need to swim those other events," Renee said.

But she had already made the team and had to swim fast again in her other events. She wanted to swim her events. She said she trained for that 800 free and wanted to swim it. That was the race that she ended up medaling in. Thank goodness she wanted to do that. The rest of the meet, she got to really just swim.

Sandeno made the team in the 800 freestyle (8:28.61), finishing behind Brooke Bennett (8:23.92) and ahead of Diana Munz (8:28.66). She also made the team in the 200 butterfly (2:09.54), finishing second to Misty Hyman (2:09.27). Sandeno barely missed making the 400 freestyle, finishing third (4:12.40), with Munz winning that event in 4:08.71.

"I ran off adrenaline the rest of the meet. The rest is pretty surreal. It all happened fast. I mean, I only started thinking about this a year ago," Sandeno said.

Now I know I worked my butt off and I know I put in the work [in and out of the water], but how does that happen? So much praise to my coaches, Vic and Renee Riggs. So much gratitude to my parents and sisters. One does not make it to the largest sporting stage in the world single-handedly.

Sandeno became the first woman since Tracy Caulkins in 1980 to qualify for an Olympic team in a freestyle, butterfly, and individual medley event. Sandeno wasn't the only U.S. teen to make the Olympics that week. Munz was just 18. Phelps made it in the 100 butterfly at age 16. Aaron Peirsol made the team in the 200 backstroke at age 17. "We were the young group," she said. "[Diana Munz and I] ended up bonding at trials and became roommates."

It started in the ready room. "Our first trials in 2000, we really connected because we were the only ones being really goofy in the ready room and everyone else was super serious—and we couldn't understand why everyone was being so serious," Munz said.

We were so young then. That was the first time we were like, "If you make the team and I make the team, we are totally roommates!" [Kaitlin] and I were so alike at how we prepped for things. Everyone prepares for races in different ways. We were both laid back, and that was the connection we had.

We saw the other side about knowing when each person had to take a nap. Don't knock on the door between this time and this time. Since we were both distance swimmers, our time line of workouts and everything was pretty similar. We were a good fit together because we were pretty open about our plan. Some athletes weren't even open about what they did because they were superstitious or just didn't want to tell the other person what they were doing. When we first met, we were so different and still so the same. Coming from Ohio and California it was different, but we both complemented each other in that way. It was fun to have another person my age. I knew the east-side people, she knew the west-side people, and we were able to connect with both sides. We were always the young girls on the team, but we could easily make friends with everyone else—and everyone kind of took us under their wings, which was awesome. That is really the swimming community in general. It was easy for the two of us to be together because there were always older ones taking us under their wings—and if there wasn't an older one, the two of us would figure out our own thing. We had each other.

It was the start of a lifelong friendship for the two teenagers, who happened to swim many of the same events. "Kaitlin and I met when we were both so young. Probably 12 or 13 when we started getting into the national circuit and swimming against each other," Munz said.

> I was from Ohio and she was from California, but we were always together. I love her. We still connect like we picked up right where we left off. She was one of those competitors that I fell instantly in love with because she was a true competitor but not one who hated everyone around them because they wanted to win. You really wanted to beat her, but you loved her at the same time—and we had a mutual relationship like that. We loved the sport. We loved to race, and when we dove in, we wanted to win. But as soon as we hit the wall it was instant laughter between the two of us. That is how we became friends and why we remained friends. To this day, if we see anyone on the pool deck that knew us when we were swimming, they would ask where our sidekick was. From that point on, we were roommates at any national meet, and we became really great friends from that point forward.

Both teenagers made the team, but they had to face off to do so. Munz made the team in the 400 free, while Kaitlin had made the 400 IM. That set up the 800 free, Munz's best event. Kaitlin managed to touch her out for second place behind Brooke Bennett to make the team. It could have been a friendship-altering situation had they not already made the team.

"I was going in thinking I was going to race the 800, and she beat me out by a couple of tenths in the 800," Munz reflected.

> I got third and she got second. We had already made the team because I made the 400 and she made the 400 IM, so we were planning on being roommates and we went into that last race. Now I was like, "Can I really be your roommate after that?!" We still joke about it today. She beat me in my main event.

Sandeno had finally wrapped her head around her stunning performance at the trials. She shared a few touching moments with her family, and then she was off. Sydney was waiting, and Sandeno, after achieving her goals for the trials, would have to quickly refocus and make some new goals for the Olympics.

The team arrived at the Olympic camp in Pasadena, California, and Sandeno was immediately placed in Coach Jon Urbanchek's group—the distance group. More accurately, the distance men.

"There was so much attention. It was such a whirlwind. It was really happening," she said.

What a blessing for me to be able to stay in Southern California for those two weeks. I was able to see family, friends, and my personal coaches while preparing for the biggest meet of my career. That is where I met and trained with legendary coach Jon Urbanchek—fondly known as Urbs or Urbie and who would remain significant all throughout my career. I ended up with Urbanchek's group, which was the distance guys. Erik Vendt, Tom Malchow, Klete Keller, and Chad Carvin. I loved it, but I hated it, being so young and picked on, in a playful manner, of course. It was like big brothers. But it was hard. Being all of 17, female, and coming from a very small club team. This was my first taste of teasing, trash-talking, next-level killer training, and instantly figuring out that I needed to put on a hard outer shell. Not to say that I didn't totally love it. I really did. I was pushed to another level in many aspects. Being more of a tomboy anyways, I was used to rolling with the guys. But now these were college guys, and they didn't let my age keep me from being the butt of most jokes. Urbs took good care of me, but boy did he train me hard. It was critical to put in long, grueling training before coming down for taper yet again. Schubert was one of the head coaches, and I remember such an aura about him. I kind of already had that feeling that I wanted to go to the University of Southern California [USC], and I kind of wanted to impress him.

It was just me, the guys, and Urbie. Urbs is just one special human being. His positive attitude is so contagious. The way he put the guys in their place but was still their best friend. The respect that everyone gave him was like nothing I had witnessed. His encouragement and how vivacious he was is out of this world. Every positive word in the thesaurus I would use for this man. Being in that training group, I was definitely the butt of every joke. They tried to get under my skin, but it made me tougher. Looking back on it, I am sure I loved it, being 17 and the only girl with all of those guys. These are guys I knew, looked up to, and thought were cute. Urbs just made it tolerable for me to get my butt kicked every day while being teased relentlessly.

That drive, along with a month of distance work with Urbanchek, had Sandeno confident as the team flew to Australia. The Olympic camp was at Pasadena, California, so not too far from Kaitlin's family and friends. They didn't get to see much of her but made the most of a few visits.

"I remember after she qualified for the Olympics and they went to camp. They were doing the camp in Pasadena, and I went up with some of her really good high school friends and her mom. We got to have lunch with her. They kind of sequester her for a month leading up to the Olympics," Bree Deters said. "She ended up showing us all the swag they got. It wasn't in a look-at-me sort of way, she was just so excited. It was jaw-dropping. I knew she was capable of it, but it was very surreal."

"She couldn't really do much because her time line was so strict, and, of course, as high school juniors and seniors, we think we are the coolest cats around. We ended up going to lunch with her," Amy Walloch said.

Leading up to it, I remember being nervous but excited. There was a lot going on. The news came to school and interviewed me. We had little cheering-her-on parties. It was kind of surreal. It just blew my mind because it was my best friend. I remember her talking about the pressure doing so many events. It was almost like she was the Michael Phelps before Michael Phelps was around. Everybody kept talking about her because she had qualified for so many events and she was so young. I remember being nervous for her because that is a lot of pressure.

Her friends weren't the only group to head to Pasadena. Coaches Vic and Renee Riggs went to the Olympic training camp to help with Kaitlin's final training before heading to Australia.

"We went first to the training camp at Pasadena. She seemed good. She certainly wasn't the youngest to ever make an Olympic team, but she was one of the youngest on the team. They put her with the boys right away, and that is where she started her relationship with Jon Urbanchek," Renee said.

She swam with the boys throughout the training trip. We flew ahead of her and met her in Brisbane. They let us come on the deck and work with her during some of those training sessions. It was certainly great for us, and I think it was good for her, too. She had never really had any other coaches during her career for a long period of time. It was reassuring to have us there, I think. She seemed ready to go. We all traveled down to Sydney.

We really felt like she had a good shot. Making the 200 fly and 800 free as well, it turned into a full-meet preparation. We were not part of the training camp in the United States, but we were part of the training camp in Australia. Within the week after trails, we left for Australia. We met with Coach Quick and turned everything over to him. We told Kaitlin that we fully trusted the Olympic staff, she just had to train hard and keep going. We then met them in Brisbane about 10 days before the games started. The team came out on deck, and we were informed by Coach Urbanchek that Kaitlin was training with the men's team. We ran a couple practices and looked at her stroke. They did a really good job of letting the club coaches or college coaches have access to their kids because it had been a problem before that in our sport, where they just kind of kicked everyone out. So we got a couple days to see how she was doing. Just by chance, I ran in to Mark Schubert, and I was able to get a training pool deck pass. Being there for her warm-up was really beneficial. Kaitlin was coming out of the gate first for her and for the United States team. I was on deck then had to get back up to my seat. It was a nervous first swim, but she made finals.

Meeting Urbanchek was one of the turning points in Kaitlin's career. She just didn't know it yet. His distance background and uncanny ability to motivate gave her something extra—something she didn't always know she had in her.

"I usually coach the middle distance and IM distance, so after we left for training camp, we went to the Gold Coast in Australia," Urbanchek said.

I really didn't know her. She was still a high school girl. Vic trusted me to take care of Kaitlin leading up to the games. Luckily Vic and Renee made it to Sydney and to the training camp, which was very important for a young girl to have a home coach. I was her coach with the rest of the 10 or so people I had in my group. She fit in right away. She got along with everybody. It was a pretty good group for me. She was the rookie. There was a lot of excitement and nervousness.

In the United States, swimming is one of the biggest Olympic sports, but in Australia, it is one of the biggest sports, period. The Americans felt more like rock stars Down Under because everyone in the host country knew about them before they even set foot on Australian soil.

Kaitlin with Coach Vic Riggs at the Sydney Olympics in 2000. *Sandeno family*

"Going to Sydney was so different. All the publicity because we were the swim team. We were a really big deal there. They bet on swimming there like it is Vegas," Sandeno said.

The first relay of the meet was the 4x100 freestyle relay, an event that the United States had performed well in throughout the years. But the U.S. men lost to Australia by a hundredth of a second. Australians rejoiced, and it looked like they were ready to dominate on their home turf. But it turned out otherwise.

Kaitlin with Coach Jon Urbanchek at the 2018 USA Swimming national championships. *Sandeno collection*

"Sydney was one of my favorites because the Australians were really tough," Urbanchek said.

They had been beating us at world championships, and that was a very exciting Games for us. The first night was the 4x100. It was a great race, and we lost by hundredths of a second. After that, Gary Hall Jr. said something like, "We are going to beat the Aussies like we beat the guitar." That Games was a parallel to a 15-round professional boxing match. The Aussies hit us with an eight count. The whole USA team got excited after that relay, and we won every round after that. We got 33 medals, and the Aussies got 13. It was an exciting experience for Kaitlin.

It was exciting but didn't quite start out that way. It was nerve-racking for the teenager. Getting to the Olympics was one thing, but performing at peak speed at the Olympics is something else altogether. It is enough to create anxiety in the head of a teenager, particularly one who was set to swim the 400 IM on the first night.

It started with simple conversation between athletes at lunch. It was one of those conversations that is harmless on the surface but can lead to a lot of pressure, especially for a swimmer preparing to compete in the first event of the Olympics. "Everybody was talking about winning medals in the cafeteria," Sandeno said.

The 400 IM being the first event meant that I had a chance to bring home the first female swimming medal. My focus then switched to Olympic medals, and that's the first time I remember getting nervous walking out to a race. The stands were completely full, and the energy was electric. I remember walking out and thinking, "Oh my gosh." But I was still smiling.

The smile quickly faded.
"The race was a nightmare," she said.

I remember going out so fast because Yana was right next to me, and she took it out so fast. It was my big rookie mistake. I didn't stick to my race plan, I raced her plan. By the breaststroke leg I was hurting. I thought I was third on the final turn. I saw "4" when I touched the wall, and I was crushed that I didn't medal. I was so upset. I felt the weight of the world on my shoulders. I didn't medal for my team, for my country. I felt like I let everyone down. I was so, so upset.

It was an emotional time for everyone in the Kaitlin Sandeno camp. It wasn't often that the constant smile and energy she portrayed seemingly at all times was erased into visible negative emotions.

"Vic was down there when she swam her 400 IM. It was amazing watching her swim that. I remember thinking that I was so proud of her. Fourth was stunning. It was amazing that she could go down there and do it," Renee said.

Vic arranged it so I could come down there and talk to her for a few minutes [since I was not on the Olympic staff], and I walked down those huge bleachers. She started to cry immediately. She was disappointed because she hadn't medaled for her team. That honestly, as a coach, it just broke my heart. I just held her and said she was the fourth fastest female in the world. You can't be disappointed in that. I wanted her to be happy. That was an achievement most people couldn't conceive of. With as little experience as she had, to do what she did was phenomenal.

That emotion was felt throughout the world as Kaitlin's friends watched from home. "I remember being so excited, then feeling bad that she finished fourth. Obviously I was super proud of her, but I had this feeling she was going to be so disappointed even though there was nothing to be disappointed about. She tends to put a lot of pressure on herself. She was so close," Amy Walloch said.

Kaitlin barely had time to wrap her head around what had happened before she was standing in front of reporters. "You have to go through the media," she said.

I was very short and not charismatic. I wanted out of there so quickly. I balled. I had never cried after a race. Vic came over and tried to calm me down. Amanda [Beard] came over to me and basically asked why I was so crushed. I told her how upset I was to finish fourth and not to medal. She goes, "You are 17 years old and only three people in the world can beat you in the 400 IM." It really changed my outlook at the international level after that. You can't let outside factors get in your head. My whole approach changed. I was always aiming for a best time after that. I had that pity party, but then my whole mentality changed. In my journal, I wrote that I felt I let my country down and my hometown down.

It took a long time for those feelings to fade. But Kaitlin didn't have a long time to get over it; she had more racing to do, starting with the 200 butterfly. It was a race Kaitlin wouldn't win, but her teammate Misty Hyman won and Kaitlin got to raise Hyman's hand like at the end of a boxing match, a moment that still makes Kaitlin break out into a huge grin.

"That race I got to hold her hand up in victory. It was one of the most iconic upsets, and I got to be a part of it celebrating with my teammate, the champ. That picture still gives me the goosebumps," she said. "It was so cool to see how my teammates reacted to that race. Everyone went absolutely crazy. Her win bonded Team USA in a special way that night. I went a best time in my race and finished sixth."

Focus shifted to the 800 freestyle, and after a rocky start, Kaitlin claimed the first Olympic medal of her career. "I had a solid second half and got my hand on the wall for a bronze. I was really happy with my time [8:24.29] and was so thrilled to be on the medal podium," she said.

> Teammate Brooke Bennett won the gold, and we got to do a lap around the pool deck with our medals to the song "Girls Just Want to Have Fun." I tried to take in every moment. It could have been my last Olympic race for all I knew. You just never know if you will qualify for the next one.

And it was a race that her roommate, Diana Munz, was planning to swim before Kaitlin ended up beating her (along with Brooke Bennett) at the Olympic trials. Despite that, their bond strengthened in Sydney—two teenagers on the world's biggest athletic stage.

"We bonded right away. It was kind of weird because we swam the same stuff and always raced each other—but I really liked her," Kaitlin said of Diana.

> I wasn't even going to do the 800 at trials, but I was having a great meet. I didn't think there was any way I was going to beat Brooke Bennett and Diana Munz. I was just swimming it to swim it. I remember during the race, I was sitting like third or fourth—I always like to back-half that race. I could see Diana, and I remember going, "Oh, crap." I really like this girl, and it was her best event. But I was having a strong race, and I could see myself catching her. I have never had that feeling ever in any of my races—and never have again. I was so competitive. But we were like best friends, and she was supposed to make it in this event. I remember just getting my hand on the wall and again going, "Oh, crap." But I remember her being very genuine in congratulating.
>
> We were attached at the hip. "Where's Diana?" "She's with Kaitlin?" "Where's Kaitlin?" "She's with Diana." We were two peas in a pod. I was her biggest fan in Sydney. I couldn't have asked for a better teammate and roommate. I give a major amount of credit to Diana for my success at the Olympics because your energy is set by the people you are around, and I was with her the whole time. I couldn't have asked for a more genuine sisterhood during the biggest swim meet of our lives.

Munz felt a sense of pride when she saw her teammate and roommate medal in the 800 free, even if it was what she thought could have been in store for herself heading into Olympic trials. "It was really fun to see her race so well. It was so empowering," Munz said. "During the 800 free, I was thinking to myself that

Kaitlin and Olympic roommate Diana Munz kiss their medals at the Sydney Olympics in 2000. *Sandeno family*

Kaitlin at the Sydney Olympics with her family and coaches. *Sandeno family*

I should be in that race, so that was hard, but I really wanted Kaitlin to medal. We were so close and such good friends that you wanted to see her walk away with a medal."

Her family was right there watching from the stands. "We had been married a couple years with no children yet, so we went to Sydney," Kaitlin's sister Camlyn said.

It was our first time traveling out of the country. We did not go to trials. That was pretty amazing to see the production of opening ceremonies.

Being there and seeing your sister's name on the board is just awesome. When she won the bronze, that was insane. Just the excitement of all of that. Seeing her from the time she was at juniors and going all the way up through college was amazing. We didn't go to a lot of big meets, but we went to the ones around here. Long Beach, great memories there. To see it all come to fruition was unbelievable.

"My brother-in-law Steve was yelling, 'Let's go San-de-no!'" Kaitlin said. And it was loud—really loud.

"That kind of started to be his thing. It started at local swim meets. He would do it right after the whistle, and finally my sister told him he couldn't do that," Kaitlin continued.

So then it happened right when I got on the blocks. It was one of those things that if I knew they were there, I would listen for it. We still laugh about it. It was very distinct. My sister is very high-pitched and I could hear her, too, but Steve could just project so you could hear it really well. It would make me smile, but I would still keep focus. It's kind of how I roll, focused but enjoying the moment. They are the best support group. I couldn't have done it without each and every one of them, and it was so cool that they were able to be there and be such a big part of it. Because of our age difference, my sisters have been with their husbands the majority of my life. They are more than just brothers-in-law; they definitely feel like my brothers.

Earning a medal, even an unexpected one, was a relief for her coaches.

"The 200 fly was great time for her. She was sixth. When the 800 came up, watching that was a little like an out-of-body experience," Renee said. "She beat her best time by a lot. I knew how excited she would be to earn a medal, and I was so excited. That is what people ask. That is what they put on TV. It is not whether it was a best time or a good performance, it was, 'Did they medal?'"

"When she got to finals, that was the first time I ever saw disappointment in the kid. It wasn't because she got fourth, it was because she felt like she let so many people down. We were like, how many people finish fourth in the world?" Vic said.

The 200 fly got her back into the meet, and that was the race where Misty Hyman broke the record. That was the year the Australians were supposed to kick the crap out of the Americans. By that time, you saw the Aussies kind of in a panic, and the Americans were swimming so well. They were talking a lot of smack beforehand, and it was a proud American moment. When I saw her face reacting to Misty's swim, I knew the 800 was going to go okay because this kid was back to being Kaitlin. Her 800 was pretty relaxed and pretty easy. Then Mark snuck me into the coach's box, and I got to watch her get a medal. It was a cool opportunity. It was one thing to come back and final in everything, and it was another thing to come back with a medal.

Despite medaling in the 800 freestyle, one of Sandeno's signature moments was in the 200 butterfly. She is forever etched in Olympic history not because she won but because of how she reacted when U.S. teammate Misty Hyman won the gold medal.

"Kaitlin didn't medal, and she was in the finals. When Misty touched the wall, she climbed over the lane lines and celebrated with her like she won herself. It plays back into that selfless person. They play it on USA Swimming videos all the time at meets," fellow swimmer Rachael Waller said.

As for the 2000 Olympics, Sandeno ended on a high note with a medal. She was starting to understand her potential and her place in the sport. Very few swimmers in history have competed in the 400 IM and the distance freestyle events—*and* the 200 butterfly. Very few.

"Nobody really swam those events like I did back then. Only a couple had ever done that. I was proud of swimming the diversity of races," Kaitlin said.

It was something even her best friends were starting to wrap their heads around. Kaitlin was a rare superstar of swimming, being able to excel in so many events.

"It was just so surreal watching her in the Olympics. I knew it was special, but it was just so weird to see my friend on TV," Bree Deters said.

I remember being younger and meeting Olympians, and thinking of them as gods and goddesses. But when Kaitlin was on TV, she was so down to earth. It was just crazy to see her on TV competing against people that you idolize. It gave me a lot of hope. When she made her first Olympic team is the same time I hit my growth spurt and my stride. It was an inspiration for sure. Even if I wasn't bound to go to the Olympics, look at what happened to her in a short amount of time. It doesn't take being a hermit and being 100 percent about training to make the Olympics. Cool things can happen. I see her being the success and celebrity that was so down to earth, and I completely feel different around sports celebrities now. They are just people. My big sister was on TV. It was one of the coolest things. I knew how cool it was, but I don't think it sunk in until she came back.

It was a blur of a week, a month, and even a year for Sandeno. There were triumphs, tribulations, disappointments, and thrills. It was a lot for a teenager to remember and put into perspective. Luckily, a school assignment helped give her a lifelong gift. "I am so glad I journaled. It was an English assignment for me. It was emotional to go back and read it," Kaitlin said.

Every time Sandeno reads her teenage musings, she remembers something different about her experience in Sydney. The thoughts of letting her country down faded as the week Down Under progressed and once Sandeno returned home. Her disappointments made her strive to produce a better performance in the years to come. Her bronze medal was a daily reminder that she wanted gold.

WORLD STAGE

Kaitlin Sandeno had achieved her goal of making the Olympics, something most athletes can only dream about. So, after coming back from Sydney in 2000, just 17 years old, the question was, Now what?

A girl who had appeared with a medal around her neck in front of the entire world was going back to finish high school. It led to plenty of anxiety about school as a teenager, already a tough time emotionally for any student. But Sandeno was coming back for her senior year as an Olympian, which was a huge extra layer on top of the stress of being a high schooler, trying to get good grades, and deciding where to go for college.

"The first week or two was insane going back to high school, which is already weird, and having the attention of being an Olympian. It was a little overwhelming," she said. "If anything, I felt like I had more of a responsibility to be a good example."

It started on her first day back.

"I had a reporter and camera crew that accompanied me to my first day of school," she said. "Imagine sitting in your civics class with a bronze medal in your backpack and a reporter in the desk next to you taking notes not on the class lecture, but on you. I wanted a break from swimming. I needed a break from swimming. A time to celebrate, refresh, and regroup."

Her family helped a lot with that, and that didn't go unnoticed. "One of the reasons she was successful is her parents didn't put a lot of pressure on her," said Mark Schubert, Kaitlin's future coach at USC and for Team USA.

I had one swimmer whose brother was on the Olympic team and won a medal, and her dad asked her what was wrong with her [because she didn't go to the

Olympics and medal] even though she was swimming her best times. After the 400 IM in 2004, I walked over to talk to Kaitlin's mom through the fence. Her mom said, "I don't know if that is a good time or not, but I am glad she is so happy." I will never forget that. She did everything for her kid to succeed but did not put pressure on. I tell that story to my parents on the first day of the season every year. It was just awesome. That is a great way to raise the child.

Her family watched as their Olympian returned to a normal daily life and a senior year of high school. "She seemed overwhelmed to me—at least at first," her mother Jill said.

Like it was a surreal experience. It all happened so fast, I don't think it ever really sunk in. There was no time to process. Like it was one thing right after the other. From the moment she qualified, to the meet, to back to school with camera crews and assemblies for her. On to homecoming queen, recruiting trips, end of senior year, prom, and, boom, off to college. But she stayed very humble and level headed. . . . But it was also the first time I had to ground her [Ha!]. She missed curfew after being out with friends at Knott's Berry Farm.

Missing curfew was a way to bring that normal teenager vibe back home. She was definitely looking to return to a normal high school experience. "She didn't flaunt it. I don't think she really liked the attention for it. Again, same old Kaitlin," her father said.

While her family was her rock, Sandeno benefitted from the fact that she wasn't defined by one group of people in high school. "I was in what was considered the 'popular group' but wasn't like 'queen bee.' I was too busy to get in trouble. I didn't have a bunch of boyfriends or anything like that. I was like the 'All-American girl,' class president, on yearbook staff, and varsity swimmer." She had her best friends but was able to connect with people from every walk of life at her school, which helped ease the transition back to high school.

In the water, there was no confusing Kaitlin, who after a month off from swimming got back in the pool training for the next step. "I would use the word *oblivious*. It didn't change her any way, shape, or form. I think we gave her a month off. We just let her be a kid. When she came back, she was the same old Kaitlin, and we had world championship trials that we started to train for," Vic said.

But Kaitlin didn't shy away from the limelight—and didn't abuse it, either. "I think she handled herself really well," friend Amy Walloch said.

I don't think people really treated her any different. I think people really liked her before she even went, so when she came back, it was amazing. She was still the

Kaitlin as homecoming queen. *Sandeno family*

same girl that everyone knew before she left. She is very down-to-earth and a normal girl. She was popular. I mean she was the president, which is something the students vote on. It is not like she was this come-from-nowhere kid in the Olympics that came back and was then all of a sudden super popular. I just remember there being more attention. The school and the town were really supportive.

Despite training for the past year for the Olympics, her schedule would get even more strenuous as she returned to high school. Classes and swimming already took up a ton of time, but now there were college visits to take and speaking engagements to attend.

"I started my senior year of high school two weeks late because of the Sydney Olympics. Upon returning to the States it felt nothing short of a whirlwind," she said.

Interviews, e-mails, phone calls, speaking engagements. Not to mention normal life. Seeing my family and friends, back-to-school shopping, prepping for the new school year. El Toro High School offered a warm welcome back. But it was anything but typical. I was gone every Friday it seemed like. Visits and swim meets. I really wanted a break from swimming. I was burned out. I did a lot of speaking engagements, and they started small, like Girl Scout troops and stuff like that. It was cool to see how supportive the community was of me.

It ended up being a positive year for Kaitlin despite the added time commitments and stress.

"Senior year was a blast," she said.

I was named homecoming queen, was school vice president, I bought my first car, and it was the first time [even though short-lived] I had a boyfriend. It was also the first time I got grounded for missing curfew. I was quickly reminded that just because you are an Olympian doesn't mean you don't have to make curfew. My family continued to keep me grounded, and my coaches got me back in the pool in order to prepare for U.S. nationals and the world championships.

Preparing for those championships meant another chance to perform with the world's best, and another chance to rekindle friendships she made in Sydney.

Meanwhile, in an age before cell phones or social media, Kaitlin had to wait to see Diana Munz until the next major swim meet. After all, Ohio and California are pretty far apart. But it never seemed that far to them. "We wanted to have fun when we went to these meets. Even when we became veterans, we tried to remind the younger kids that the reason they started swimming was because it was fun. That is what a lot of people forget, and it is a spirit Kaitlin and I always wanted to keep alive," said Munz.

> That was something that we love together. There are so many serious moments with training and racing that people forget to have fun. As soon as we left, we were like, "See you at trials for Pan Pacific Games," and nationals was like six months later. We were young enough that we really didn't take a break. For us, it was like, "What meet are you going to?" There were so many in line that it never seemed like that long before we saw each other again. I think it would be a completely different relationship if there were cell phones then. That would have been awesome.

But it was only a matter of time before their next big moment in the pool—and again it would be together.

5

TROJAN LIFE

K aitlin Sandeno had just started to get used to the fact that she was back in high school after competing in the Olympics. Things were just getting back to normal—at least as normal as they could get as a teenager with an Olympic medal—when it was time to prepare for college. Selecting a school that is the best fit can be extremely difficult for anyone, but when athletics are added into the mix, it can be a nightmare. There are so many factors to consider, between academics, location, the team, the coach, the athletic facilities, and the traditions.

Kaitlin was on everyone's radar after making the Olympic team as a high school swimmer. Once recruiting officially opened for her class, she was a hot commodity. More than one hundred schools sent her information and showed interest in signing her. Coaches knew that despite her incredible success at a young age, her fastest, most successful days in the pool were still ahead of her. She had her pick of pretty much any school in the country. It was a stressful time for Kaitlin, but she was slowly able to narrow down her choices to three heading into her senior year at El Toro High School and take control of a situation that oftentimes takes control of the athlete.

"I ended up taking only three recruiting trips my senior year," Kaitlin said.

I also decided that I was going to sign late as well. I felt too rushed upon returning from Sydney. I visited University of Georgia, University of Arizona, and University of Southern California. I always had a feeling that I would be a USC Trojan but was definitely open-minded to other schools. I knew the swim program was a good match for me and what a legend I would be swimming for Coach Mark Schubert. Schubert also coached my club coach, Vic Riggs, so I felt like I already had an idea of the training I would be doing at USC.

There were some obvious advantages to USC, one of them being remaining on the West Coast. "I liked being close enough to home, as I was not ready to venture too far from my parents and comfort zone," Kaitlin added. "I was honored, humbled, and grateful to accept a full ride scholarship and proudly sported my USC sweatshirt upon signing."

It was a proud moment for the Sandeno family, as well as USC and Coach Schubert. "She swam [800 free and 400 IM] the events that we had a lot of people she could train with. That was a big attraction for her. I don't know if the coaching had anything to do with it, but I'd like to think that it did a little bit," Schubert said with a chuckle.

> Her club coach swam for me at Mission Viejo, and I think that helped. We had quite a few people that had been to the Olympics on our team, so she wasn't the only one coming in at that level, which probably made her feel more comfortable. The team expectation was that everyone was striving for that level.

The excitement of a new challenge and a new place was intoxicating. Everything was brand new, and the possibilities were endless. "I thought my first week of college was the greatest thing ever," Kaitlin said.

> I was having a total blast. Meeting my new teammates, being in the dorms, meeting other athletes—it was incredible. But quickly the reality of how challenging it was going to be to juggle swimming, academics, social life, and everything in between set in. I missed my parents, I missed swimming on my club team. Before I knew it, I was struggling in my classes and was dealing with a shoulder injury. I felt tired all the time and wanted nothing more than to take a nap instead of attend class. I was eating unhealthy and staying up too late. I didn't notice it then, but looking back now at old photos I put on a lot of weight, which obviously didn't help my swimming. College was hard. It was really hard my first semester. It was such a huge change for me. It didn't help that I had a shoulder injury right when the season started. So I had to be in the training room and miss our first meet. It made it really challenging. I remember loving my first week of college, and by the second week, I was so homesick. That first week, you are meeting people, meeting your team, going to socials. School was hard for me. I am more street smart than I am book smart. My mind goes a hundred different ways.

It was a new kind of frustrating. "I called my mom and I was like, 'I am the dumbest person here,'" she said.

> Morning workouts were killing me. I needed sleep. I missed classes because I was so tired. I got some bad grades. I had to get the athletic tutoring. Good for USC

for not letting that stuff slide. It took me a while to adjust emotionally and physically. In December of my freshman year, I had excruciating back pain and didn't know where it was coming from. That started a very long process.

Meanwhile, Kaitlin reached out to family and friends at home for support, while trying to maintain a somewhat normal college life. "We were always together. So when we left for college, we were still trying to maintain that," childhood friend Amy Walloch said.

So there were a lot of calls just seeing how the other was doing. How is college? How are classes? Did you meet any boys? We would e-mail and talk on instant messenger. It was really keeping in touch with life, what we were doing, who we were dating, what we were majoring in. That still happens to this day.

Unfortunately, the usual battles of a college student, especially an athlete, began to take a toll. Kaitlin continued,

That freshman 15 for me was like 25 pounds, and it definitely was not muscle. I was always hungry when I was training. Then it was a back injury. It didn't get diagnosed until after NCAAs in March. It literally took my breath away it was so painful. We went to every doctor and had every test, and some of them were super painful. It was the first time that I felt like I hated swimming. I had those moments in high school after a long day, but I would never give up. There were definitely times my freshman year of college where I wanted to quit. It almost made me feel like I was lying about it because no one could figure out what was wrong with me. Am I crazy? There is a pain that is taking my breath away, and every specialist in L.A. can't figure it out. I tried to swim through it. I still made NCAAs, and I don't really know how. At NCAA, we tried taping my ribs in place so I wasn't swimming in so much pain. Needless to say, trying to race a 200 butterfly constricted like that was absolutely awful. I wanted to rip it off mid-race.

Somehow, Kaitlin still managed to turn in an All-American performance at the NCAA championships. It was so painful she considered quitting the sport altogether. "It often crossed my mind," she told the *Orange County Register* before the NCAAs in 2003. "But I wasn't going to give up without a fight." She added,

I recall trying to get through the warm-up but literally couldn't move without pain. I tried to go about my day, but I could not kick the pain. This was the start of a very long and frustrating, nearly career ending, injury. Schubert kindly reminded me of the importance of being honest about things like this because I was reluctant to share this injury at first but was optimistic that I would overcome

Kaitlin gets set to race at the 2004 NCAA championships. *Peter H. Bick*

this. He was right, but it took until the end of my junior year to finally be pain free. Not to mention six months to even get a diagnosis. Doctor after doctor. Specialist after specialist. Test after test. No one knew what was wrong with me for quite some time. I continued to swim as much as I could bear while going through this wild goose chase. I surprisingly still made it to the NCAA's but didn't accomplish anything impressive in my mind. It wasn't until returning from NCAA's I finally got answers. The day I got back I got an imaging that showed a stress fracture in my back. I had a stress fracture in my intercostal muscles. They were like, "No swimming." I had never not been in the water. I needed to completely stop swimming, attend hours of physical therapy to allow this to heal. I had never taken so much time out of the pool.

For someone who had been constantly in the water for more than a decade, it was more than jolting. It was life-altering. Kaitlin could not get in the water. She could only rest and recuperate. She had plenty of time to think about everything she had accomplished and everything she hadn't yet. There were countless hours where the dark thoughts of doubt could creep in. How big of an injury is this, really? Am I ever going to get back in the water? Are my best days behind me? Will I still love the sport when I finally get back in the water? How much pressure will I put on myself when I return? The maddening carousel of questions marinated in Kaitlin's mind for months.

"I had asthma and coughed a ton, and that pulled my intercostals apart, which is where my stress fracture was, so it never could heal. It was a two-part thing. I had to get my asthma taken care of so it could heal. It was slow progress," Kaitlin said.

I was out of the water and just doing physical therapy, two to three hours a day, and that was my day. It was an emotionally hard time in my life, but at the same time, it was a little bit of a nice break from swimming. I swam on and off through my freshman year with it, then took the entire summer off before my sophomore year.

It was a challenge she was willing to face head-on, but she needed some help. "Nick Theders, my physical therapist—he would give up his lunch break and go to the pool with me, and give me a snorkel and see how much I could do. It was usually like 200. A 300 was a good day. I was crawling back into being in shape."

While some things were moving at a crawling pace, others were racing. Kaitlin had somehow finished her first year of college and her first year on the team at USC. Things would be different as a sophomore. "I went back for my sophomore year and got out of the dorms, which was good for me. I had a good living situation with three water polo guys. My teammates were right next door. It was perfect. I slowly tried to get my mileage back up."

She also met a kindred spirit who joined her team that year, Kammy Miller. "We met briefly on my recruiting trip. The morning after I graduated from high school, I moved to L.A. so I could begin training immediately. We hit it off as soon as she got to school," Miller said.

One of the reasons I was drawn to USC was because I didn't have a big team growing up and I was excited to be on that platform. I felt comfortable on my recruiting trip because of our personalities. I obviously knew who Kaitlin was. There was never an air of her being a teenage superstar. She was outgoing and warm and welcoming.

The similarities between Kaitlin and Kammy began to pile up. Kammy continued,

We are each one of three girls. We are both super, super tight with our families. We bonded over that. We have a lot of common ground and created a lot of fun out of that common ground. We refer to each other as soul sisters. I didn't really know what to expect. We had the Olympic coach as our coach and a handful of Olympians. She [Kaitlin] has this effervescence about her that is contagious and infectious. It is like we were instantaneously sisters. It was really just an honor more than anything to be joining USC. I cancelled my other recruiting trips because I knew I fit in, and it was more a personality thing than anything.

Then there was the adjustment to training with a team full of Olympians. Kammy quickly found out how pivotal Kaitlin's role would be in helping not only her, but also the entire team by leading by example. Kammy further stated,

Overall, it was a very intense training atmosphere. She always rose to whatever challenge we had in practice. She took it very seriously but always managed to have a complete blast doing it.

Swimming was everything to all of us at that point. It didn't matter what the challenge was or how bad she was hurting, but she always managed to rise—always. That was something that I admired as a friend and as a fan. She would be so amazing in the water and get out of the water and was just a regular person. She brought her A game to practice, that's for sure. And she brought her A+ game to meets.

That is what fellow Olympian Lindsay Benko (Mintenko) remembers about Kaitlin as well. Benko was ahead of Kaitlin in school and graduated from USC

Kaitlin (right) with Kammy Miller in London for the 2012 Olympics as fans. *Sandeno collection*

before Kaitlin got there, but she still trained with the postgraduate group at USC. "I remember meeting her in '99. I was just finishing up my college career," said Lindsay.

> I swam with her as a postgrad at USC when she was in school. It was really special. Our lanes were so full. After Sydney, when we were training for Athens, there were eight people in a lane and getting lapped before we started swimming. There were so many people training to be part of an Olympic team. That was really special to be a part of. Kaitlin brings an energy to everything that she does. It is always fun to have new faces come in and challenge you.

That was the feeling for Kaitlin's competition as well, especially in the Pac-10. "I had always known her from being California swimmers, then her at USC and me at Cal," 12-time Olympic medalist Natalie Coughlin said. "We didn't really swim too much of the same events, but I raced 200 fly a lot my freshman year and sophomore year. I did the 200 fly more in the dual-meet format more than anything those first two years. So I raced Kaitlin in those types of events."

After months of getting her body prepared for competing at the highest level in the pool, one moment almost undid everything. It was a moment that Sandeno will never forget. Sandeno and her future roommate, Kammy Miller, were lucky to be alive. The two of them were taking a couple of teammates to the Long Beach Airport on a Friday night leading into spring break—just days before the Trojans were set to leave for the NCAA championships.

"I asked Kaitlin to go with me so [on the way back] I could stay in the carpool lane and cut the trip in half [traffic-wise]," Kammy said.

> We were one exit away from being back at school in the carpool lane. I was on the left side of two lanes. I think she was reading a magazine. You have to come up because the carpool lane rises above the freeway. There was a construction barrel in the middle of the road that had fallen over. There were cars all around me and no shoulder.

Kammy is able to look back at every millisecond now and break down what happened, but at the time, it all happened so fast that it was a complete blur to both her and Kaitlin. Coming up the hill, the car was on a collision course with the construction barrel. Instincts tell you to move out of the way of a collision, so that is what Kammy did.

"Having just turned 19 two nights before, I didn't have the same driving experience. I should have just hit the barrel head on. My car could have sustained that. You couldn't really see what was in front of you until you were right there. I tried to avoid it and overcorrected," she said.

My car just kept spinning and hitting and spinning and hitting and spinning and hitting. Somehow by the grace of God I did not touch another vehicle or hurt anyone but myself. My car stayed upright. I was in a very big, safe car. But the damage caused by the seatbelt and the airbag and the steering column trapped my arm during all of this spinning and injured me severely.

"[Kammy] swerved and we hit the center rail, bounced off, and hit it again. I don't know how we didn't hit another car; it is one of the busiest freeways there is," Kaitlin said.

The car was totaled. I called my parents. I swear my parents were there in what felt like 15 minutes, although there's no way it was under an hour that time of day. I remember seeing something in the road and being a backseat driver [actually a side-seat driver] and telling her to watch out. It looked like a trash can. She went to avoid it and just overexaggerated the turn to dodge it and just lost control. It just happened so quickly. We spun around and hit the front, then spun back, and hit the back; it was almost like a pinball. Thank God she had a massive car. I saw it coming. Then I felt bad because I wondered if I freaked her out. But I wasn't screaming or anything because it was in the distance. It happened so fast. I don't remember much of what happened afterward. We were really shaken up. The biggest thing to me was: How did we not hit another car? This was one of the busiest freeways in L.A. How was there nobody else there? To this day, I still wonder. The airbags went off, and it hurt my face and my ears. I had a weird sensation in my ears. I remember looking at Kammy to see if she was okay. I remember checking my body to see if I was bleeding. I opened my door, and that freaked me out because liquid was running under the car and I thought it was blood. And I was like, "Holy crap is Kammy okay?!"

Kaitlin was banged up, but it was far worse for Kammy.

"I was fortunate that we both walked away from the car. I had to kick my door open to get out," Kammy said.

My eyes were bruised. My arms were bruised. My chest was bruised. I looked awful. I was severely hurt. It ended up being a career-ending injury for me. They took us to the pool the next morning to see if we could swim. We are both levelheaded from levelheaded families. We always had a strong friendship and got through a lot of tough things together. It was just something that happened.

Then it was time for another set of a million questions to creep into San-
deno's mind. How did this happen? How hurt am I? How hurt is everyone else?
Can I swim at NCAAs this week? Why does this stuff keep happening to me?
Thankfully, it was mostly bumps and bruises to go along with the shell shock.

"My main concern was their health and ability to compete after something
like that. Going through a lot of injuries and being the person she was, I think
she [Kaitlin] knew she could come out of it okay. Was I upset? Yes, the best
swimmer getting hurt before the meet affects the team," Coach Mark Schubert
said. "It was just bad timing. Using Murphy's law, it is going to catch up with
you sometime."

They both could swim, at least enough to want to compete for a national
championship.

"The doctor told us in a week or two we would be okay. We were like,
NCAAs is in three days, and he said there was no reason we couldn't swim, it
would just be really painful," Kammy said.

The meet was at Auburn that year, and once we got there I got super sick. I had
a 102 fever and remember just shivering with my parka on laying on the massage
table. It was just one thing after another. I swam average. My cap came off during
the mile. I felt like somebody was telling me to stop swimming.

While it ended up becoming a career-ending injury for Kammy, the end
wasn't immediate. She went with Kaitlin to swim at nationals.

"I still competed at NCAAs a few days later. Neither of us did as well as
we could have done. But we were still both All-Americans, and I think we got
third," Kammy related.

I kept swimming into my sophomore year through excruciating back pain. I at-
tempted to rehab and saw doctor after doctor. It was my number-one priority
because it was all I wanted to do. We got to a point where I did everything I
could, and the doctor told me I couldn't do this anymore. I remember going up
to Schubert's office to tell him that, which was awful. He said he had never seen
someone try harder to come back from an injury than I did. So I had that closure
and peace of mind.

But there is not the same closure with Kammy's body. "To this day, I struggle with the pain in my back that I sustained," she said. "I still see a doctor every
Wednesday morning at 7 a.m. to manage the severe pain that has not subsided
since March of 2003."

Even with going through all of those years of pain and anguish, Kammy is quick to point out that it could have been worse for her—and Kaitlin.

"I don't think it was necessarily a turning point in either one of our lives. Fortunately, it did not hurt Kaitlin. That would have been awful," she said.

It is not something we really dwelled on as friends, which I am grateful for. We were already super close. I think had the roles been reversed and she was the one with career-ending injuries and I was the one who walked out unscathed, I'm sure there would have been a different outcome. I can't fathom being the cause of somebody else's pain like that [and I am so glad I don't have to].

While Kaitlin's issues stemming from the accident were minuscule in comparison to Kammy, it was still jolting and still a big deal. It was one more thing she had to overcome throughout her career at USC.

How do you bounce back from that? It takes a clear mind and a big heart. Kaitlin had dealt with a shoulder injury, a back injury, the adjustment to college, and a car accident, while fighting through asthma, which tweaked her back with each cough. Those asthma attacks can quickly turn into bronchitis, which can be detrimental to a swimmer. How many more things would Kaitlin have to deal with—and was it worth it to continue to swim?

"There were so many times I wanted to give up, but, ultimately, I had a full-ride scholarship. I wanted to get that degree, and I wasn't ready to give up on that," she said. "Plus I still wanted to make the Olympics again."

Pain can end careers, but it can also motivate athletes to push through it. In this case, pain drove Kaitlin to even more success at USC and a summer of the best swimming of her life.

NCAA TITLES

As the deck seemed more stacked against her by the day, Kaitlin Sandeno reached the first real crossroads of her career heading into her junior season at USC. She had already accomplished so much in the water, but injuries were starting to take a toll. How motivated could she be to continue to swim when she was seemingly in constant pain and, on top of that, barely able to breathe because of chronic asthma?

"The injuries and illnesses were just really hard. I had a hard time rebounding. If it wasn't one thing, it was another. Looking back, I was proud of how I handled everything," Sandeno said.

But it didn't feel like an accomplishment in the moment, when everything was a frustrating struggle. Day by day, Sandeno hung in there as she searched for the motivation to keep going. She knew she didn't want to leave the sport in a heap of injuries. She wanted to go out her own way. Most people affected by injuries don't have that choice. But in her mind, there was plenty of unfinished business. Kaitlin wanted to have a successful, somewhat healthy college season, and she wanted to make another Olympic team.

In July 2003, Kaitlin competed in the annual Janet Evans Invitational, and while most swimmers use the meet as a chance to experiment with new techniques while training for a bigger meet or have a fun meet with nothing on the line, Kaitlin turned heads with her raw speed, something not expected for this meet. She won the 200 butterfly in 2:09.72. It wasn't a record, but for an unrested swimmer recovering from injuries, it was an astonishingly good sign. "I was shocked," she told the *Los Angeles Times* after the race. "It's kind of scary. My coach asked me, 'How are you going so fast right now?'"

It was a turning point that launched the peak of Kaitlin's career.

And it started with something small that got her motivated. "Junior year, I was elected captain. It was a huge honor. I wasn't swimming really well, so I thought it spoke to my leadership abilities and character. I was a work-hard and race-hard person, not a rah-rah person," she said.

> Junior year was strong. I felt like Mark Schubert and I had a great relationship my junior year. He could have easily been like, "This girl is a mess." But he never gave up on me. It turns out, my junior year NCAAs was a meet I was waiting so long to have. Finally. I felt really accomplished and finally satisfied with how a meet went.

Part of the season was spent fully embracing her "soul sister," Kammy Miller. The two moved into an apartment together, which provided a much-needed escape from everything—swimming, school, team drama, boy drama, you name it.

"It was really balanced. It was a place to come home to. At the height of her career, it was a sense of normalcy. It was kind of a sanctuary for her in a sense. We were living together when she went pro. I had a front row seat to those Olympics," Kammy said.

> Being able to create a sense of normalcy, peace and quiet, and comfort in our apartment on Ellendale was just kind of regular. That is why it worked. Maybe it was refuge for her. It was a way to get away from everything else bubbling up outside. What allowed us to be close roommates is that we had similar interests and aesthetics. Everything was on the same page.

But it took an entire season of getting healthy and, at the same time, high-level training to approach the level of swimming Kaitlin knew she was capable of. Slowly, she began to see her old form—and opponents saw it, too.

One race stands out to Kaitlin. It was in a dual meet between USC and Cal, in the 200 free—not the signature event of either elite swimmer. But this race was different. Coach Schubert put Kaitlin in the outside lane to kind of hide her in the race, like somehow she could feel like she was sneaking up on Natalie Coughlin. But both teams were well aware of what was happening by the time Kaitlin got on the blocks.

"I will never forget the swim meet Cal versus USC. It was my junior year. I was finally strong in the pool. Cal came, and Schubert was going to mix it up a little bit and put me in the 200 free against her," Kaitlin reflected.

> And he put me in an outside lane. I kind of walked to the blocks a little bit behind. It was going to be a showdown. She beat me, of course, but it was a really

good race. Then I had to step up and swim another race in like 10 minutes. I was worse. Trying to beat her in that first race took everything out of me. It is funny because my relationship with Natalie has changed so much. We are originally from a similar area. We are close in age. We pretty much did all the same races growing up. She was on this team the Terrapins, and it was always like, "Oh, this Natalie girl again." I have known her forever, and we have raced forever. She was really great, then phased out a little bit and I came on a little bit, then she came on again and dominated the sport. At that point, we really didn't swim the same events much, maybe once or twice in college.

Racing against the best in the world, like Coughlin, helped. So did another factor, something Kaitlin didn't realize until later. During this time, Sandeno was in a long-distance relationship. It was something that had taken a toll on her, but during this year, it turned out to be just what she needed.

"It curbed my social life. I wasn't going out as much or as late. I think that had something to do with it," she said.

But I know it was because I really wanted it. I wanted a year to be proud of. I was running out of NCAA's to make a statement at, to live up to my full-ride scholarship. I would have liked to accomplish a little bit more at USC, but it is what it is, and I don't have any regrets. I feel like I had a well-balanced experience and an experience I can use to help mentor others.

Part of it was being well-balanced in the pool. "At USC, coach would tell her she needed to work on breaststroke for the IM because that was her weakest stroke. In my head, I am thinking, man, that was the first event she ever qualified for juniors in," said childhood friend Bree Deters, who was also a USC teammate of Kaitlin.

There was a point where the butterfly was her weakest stroke. I remember a time when I was maybe 12 and we were swimming the 200 fly. I think it was the first time we had swam that, and I was in her heat. If I didn't beat her, I was really close. We were about the same that race. Then two years later, that is the event she is going to the Olympics in. That was probably one of those events she had to swim that she didn't want to swim. Then sure enough, she made two Olympic teams with it.

That didn't come without an exorbitant amount of work. The workouts were tough at an elite NCAA program. Kaitlin had practice at 6 a.m. every weekday morning except Wednesday. She then went to class and tried to find time to eat and rest before heading back for afternoon practice.

"I did morning classes, so I went straight from the pool to the classroom," she said.

I took a full load of classes. Then I always tried to get a nap in there somewhere before lunch, then it was back on the pool deck at 1:45 p.m. with practice from 2 to 4, then from practice to the weight room for about an hour. Then I had a lot of shoulder work done in the training room. I also had study table or a tutor, then eat dinner, do homework, and go to bed. That was my schedule during the week.

It didn't get any less hectic on the weekends because that is when most meets were, or a 7 to 10 a.m. Saturday practice, and that was followed by recruits coming to campus.

It was kind of interesting because she had a good hand in getting me to USC. She hosted me on my recruiting trip. When the Olympic year happened, she was definitely more down to business. I feel like while she was involved in the team stuff, she kept a healthy distance as much as she could, too. We were at school together, but it wasn't the time that we were the closest. There was a lot going on and a lot of pressure for her, not just to perform for USC, but to make the Olympics again. She hadn't really had a good NCAAs up to that point. The past couple of years had been kind of rough, then she just kind of had the meet of her life. I was so happy for her.

Because of Kaitlin's "curbed" social life, she made different weekend decisions during her junior year, in particular. "If there wasn't a football game or recruits visiting or a meet, I went home to my parents' house," she said. "I was like 70–30 going home maybe. I mentally needed that—I really did. That is the biggest reason I picked USC. It was close enough so I could do that."

On the team, she started to grow closer to her teammates, building lasting friendships that continue to this day. One of the biggest connections was with Erik Vendt.

"Erik Vendt and I really became close my junior year. He actually lived with me after the 2004 Olympics, sleeping on the couch, because he thought he had graduated but he had one more class," she said.

Later on, he came to Michigan with me. He was like the brother I never had. He literally went through everything with me. Highs, lows, everything in between. It was special. We went to the Olympics together. He was an important part of my career. I needed him so bad in Ann Arbor because I was so miserable for part of it. But having him there was like having a piece of home there with me. He was my best friend. [Meanwhile] Joanna [Jo] Fargus was my bestie, connected at the hip. She was born in England, swam for England in the Olympics. She broke her ankle her junior year and never really recovered, which was unfortunate. Kammy Miller, my friend from [the state of] Michigan. We were roommates and great friends to this day. And Heather Vallerio. She was my big sister on the team that took me under her wing.

Kaitlin, in turn, was that person for swimmers like Bree Deters and Rachael Waller.

"Growing up in Kansas City, swimming is not huge there," Rachael said.

I knew who she was because she was a big name in swimming. I always looked up to her. She is part of why I went to USC. We joke about that now because she is one of my best friends, but when I was like 14, 15 years old, I did an art project. It was a black-and-white drawing of a picture. I chose a picture of her. Yeah are you kidding me? She was my idol. It was so embarrassing when I met her. I was nervous to meet her. I came through recruiting the fall of 2004. Schubert had all the Olympians come down to his place for a barbecue with the team and the recruits. I had just watched them on TV and was playing beach volleyball with them. It was so cool. You never know what you are going to get after watching people on TV. She is so genuine. That is not the same across the board. By the time most kids are seniors, they are not really engaged in the recruiting process. But she cared, and she was part of the spirit. She was always proud of the USC tradition and proud to be a Trojan. She was leading by her actions. I don't think anything changed in that aspect when she went pro.

What was it that made Kaitlin such a draw to Waller, Deters, and a slew of others? "Her energy is what I remember," Waller said.

You have some leaders who lead by being vocal, others by simply their actions. It is clear when you see her that she wasn't trying to put up a front. She was unapologetic about her energy. She was leading the team by her times and also her bubbly personality. She was very naturally talented. I have seen some Olympians that worked very hard and others who kind of coasted on talent. She definitely worked really hard. She competed in the hardest races of all of them and did it with a smile on her face. That speaks volumes to who she is and her approach to everything.

Then there was the coaching. "Schubert was a big part of my career," Kaitlin said.

My first experience was with Schubert on the 2000 Olympic team. I remember being really impressed by him. He was intimidating but approachable. You wanted

Kaitlin (right) and Rachael Waller at a USC football game. *Sandeno collection*

to swim well for him. That was my first experience. I thought it would be awesome to swim there. Vic had swum for him, too, so I knew that would be similar.

Kaitlin's former club coach, Vic Riggs, joined the staff, too. "Mark asked if he could interview me for the assistant job, and I was offered the job. You run into two concerns. I wanted to make sure the rest of the team felt like I was capable of coaching them," Vic commented.

The interesting aspect of all of that is I never got the sense that it was looked upon like that because I was not really leading Kaitlin's group very much in practice that first year. It was a fun reunion, and it got me into college coaching. That was a goal of mine. That Olympic year, I can tell you I was part of one of the most amazing practices I have ever been a part of. I remember Kaitlin went off. Erik

Vendt went off. Lindsay Benko went off. Kalyn Keller was sub-4:20 in something in practice. It was a crazy practice. That is kind of when we thought we weren't going to just get one kid on the team, we might get a bunch of kids on the team. Kaitlin's college career absolutely was a struggle. She was doing what she needed to do, and it all kind of came together at NCAAs. It was the same process. She got healthy, and she was training well, not overexerting herself. Mark did not accept anything below a certain level, and you heard about it if you weren't there. Her NCAA led to the confidence of everything she did at trials.

Everything was starting to piece together. Sandeno was healthy, both mentally and physically; had a great and growing relationship with her teammates and coaches; had enough time to spend with her family; and was starting to crank out strong midseason times in the water. She had every reason to be optimistic.

Sandeno could slowly see the gears turning, even in everyday training. "I had finally been able to get back to hard training and did well in my workouts," she said.

Physically, I had felt behind because of my injury, but also mentally. I had never experienced that before. I finally reached a place where my mental strength was back. I am a huge believer in the difference between a good and great athlete being your mind-set. I felt like I needed that component to swim like I was able to. I needed a couple of great races for my confidence to return.

The Pac-10 championships was one of those meets. Sandeno won the 400 freestyle (4:05.74) and the 200 butterfly (1:52.63), good enough for USC and Pac-10 conference meet records. She finished runner-up in the 200 IM and looked poised for a big finish to her season.

"She was very encouraging to people who needed encouragement. I always believe in setting leadership through example. Nobody did a better job of that than her. Not only did she have to swim with injuries, but when she was healthy, nobody was better than her at training," Schubert said.

The 2004 NCAA championships were hosted by Texas A&M in College Station, Texas. Sandeno was coming off of a stellar Pac-10 performance and began preparing for her quest of a national championship with a lot of rest and, hopefully, a strong taper.

In Olympic years, the NCAA meets used to be in short-course meters format, a different length of the pool than short-course yards the other years.

Kaitlin didn't disappoint. Sandeno won the 400 IM in one of the most dominating college swims of all time, finishing in 4:30.44, which broke the American, U.S. Open, NCAA, Pac-10, and USC records—and that was just

Kaitlin being congratulated by her mother after winning the NCAA title. *Sandeno family*

the beginning. She broke every one of those except the American record in the 200 IM (2:08.11) to earn her second national championship. She closed out the meet by taking second in the 200 butterfly, at 2:06.02. She was the individual high scorer at the NCAA championships.

"Her strokes were awesome. I wouldn't say flawless, I would say awesome," USC coach Mark Schubert said. "Somehow, I would never see it in practice, but she was able to put it together and go fast in the breaststroke. I have never seen her swim backstroke that well. At the NCAAs, it was more about the competition and not to have anyone beat her."

"I broke the American record in the IM, then the last day I got outtouched in the 200 butterfly by Mary Descenza and I wouldn't talk to anyone else the rest of the night after that final race. I was so pissed," Kaitlin said.

> It was two-tenths. I was so upset. It gives you a little glimpse at how competitive I was. People were like, "You had an awesome meet!" and I was like, "I can't believe I got second in the fly." I was so angry at myself. But it was my only good NCAA meet. You look at my college career and it wasn't that great. It wasn't glamorous, but my USC days definitely shaped me. Coach was always talking about never giving up, then fast forward to my role with the Jessie Rees Foundation and their slogan being "NEGU," Never Ever Give Up. That was the epitome of my college career.

It was a proud moment for Schubert, who had watched Kaitlin go through and overcome so many obstacles. "The NCAA meet is what we focus on for the college season," he said.

She had not really had the success I knew she could have. She just dominated that meet. I think we weren't surprised because she was so determined to have a meet like that. It was very gratifying. She is just a tremendous racer. Whether things are going perfectly or not, she is going to race. That was what was so much fun about coaching her. It was her attitude. Sometimes she would come in kind of discouraged, but overall she stayed pretty optimistic. She is a very confident person. She was a lot more of a mature athlete from a confidence standpoint. She didn't flaunt it, but everyone knew every time she stepped on the blocks she expected to win. The main thing was to just stay positive and have her feel my confidence in her.

Kaitlin standing on the podium after winning an NCAA championship for USC. *Peter H. Bick*

To keep her in the same mentality when she was healthy. It wasn't perfect every day, but she did a great job of that.

It turns out she would be ending her college career on a high note because Sandeno was headed for the professional ranks just in time for the Olympic trials. "NCAAs helped my Olympic trials so much. That was the meet I needed for trials. It was a pretty monumental meet for my mental state," she said. Especially with the thoughts of the possibility of going pro on her mind.

She was back, and there was only one question remaining: Could anything derail her chances of making another Olympic team?

7

ROAD TO ATHENS

A ll it took was having a healthy year to show what Kaitlin Sandeno could do. After years packed with injuries, trials, and tribulations, she finally proved she was still one of the best swimmers in the country, earning an NCAA championship in multiple individual events months after having to miss the world championships because of injury. She made it through all of those college trials; now it was time to prove to the world what she could do at the Olympic trials.

Kaitlin was no longer the teen phenom, the swimmer everyone was eyeing. Even with her NCAA titles, Kaitlin was up against much more than college competition at the Olympic trials. It turned out to be an almost perfect scenario for Kaitlin, who has always embraced the role of underdog. The pressure was off, but the determination was on, making her a dangerous, under-the-radar threat in a multitude of events.

"Coming off a successful NCAA was a huge confidence boost going into the summer of the 2004 Olympic trials. Even though I had an awesome championship meet, I still felt I was considered a dark horse to make the Olympic team, and I actually liked that," Kaitlin said.

Going into the 2000 Olympic trials, I felt like I had so many eyes on me with a target on my back. The 2004 Olympic trials were the complete opposite. In 2000, I was confident, but in 2004, I was just grateful to be there. I really wanted to break 4:40 in the 400 IM. I didn't have a ton of expectations on myself this year, and I was kind of under the radar and I liked that. I was just stoked that I actually qualified for the trials, which seemed like a long shot just a summer before that. I liked being under the radar this time around. I had a solid summer of meets leading up to trials, but the meet right before trials was absolutely awful. I was so far off my times and felt so tired and sluggish in the water.

Taper is a dangerous time mentally for swimmers, especially if they feel sluggish. It is so easy to feel slow in the water and doubt everything, from the process to one's own ability. Kaitlin was in the middle of that leading up to trials. But for her, there were plenty of other things creeping into her mind, especially the injuries. Was she sluggish because she was not fully healthy? Was she behind the pace of other tapers? What could that mean? Kaitlin was somehow able to get through and focus on the end of taper.

"I was definitely ready for a big taper," she said.

Leading up to trials, I felt strong during taper and was at ease emotionally. I was honestly just grateful to be competing. Obviously, the ultimate goal was to make my second Olympic team, but I really just wanted to race hard and see time improvements. And more than anything, I wanted to break the 4:40 barrier in the 400 IM.

While the scenario of being the underdog was almost perfect, the location of the trials was nothing short of perfection for Kaitlin. The 2004 Olympic trials were in Long Beach, California, not far from her home. It meant familiarity with the surrounding area, and, more importantly, it meant everyone in her support group—family and friends, neighbors and former teammates—could be there.

"I could not be happier to be competing so close to my childhood hometown. I had many meets growing up in Long Beach, and I always swam well there. There was just something about that town," she said.

Being that it was so close, I had so many family and friends at the trials, my forever support system, loud and large in number rooting me on. That first night was the 400 IM. Being in Long Beach, it is 40 minutes from home. My whole family was there and friends and neighbors. It was sunny, beautiful, on the water. Everything about it was magical.

Kaitlin again had a big first day at the trials, competing in the 400-meter individual medley. For four years, Kaitlin had been chasing a time she couldn't quite reach. Every time she swam the event, she was thinking about breaking 4:40. She had been close many, many times and was hoping that in front of her family and friends, she would finally see a 4:39 on the scoreboard next to her name. She would finish second in the event to make the Olympic team, but it was a mix of emotions. As Kaitlin looked up at the scoreboard, she saw 4:40 again. Really? Again?!

"On the first day, it was the 400 IM," Kaitlin continued.

Katie Hoff went flying right by me on the breaststroke leg to take away my lead, and I was like, "Who is this girl?" I felt good until that point and I ended up second—and I was legit pissed, 4:40 again. I was happy to have made it, but I was like seriously, 4:40 again? Mary Wagner from USA Swimming told me she never saw someone so upset at making the Olympic team. Then it really set in. I couldn't believe it happened after the way the last couple of years had gone. I was excited and pissed.

I wanted to break that barrier so badly. But hey, I was going to my second Olympics," she said, knowing the chance would come to break that barrier in Athens.

I had overcome all my adversities the past four years and was going to Athens. As I got out of the water, I explained I had one ultimate goal—break 4:40—and that did not happen today. But needless to say, I brushed that off and enjoyed the moment. I embraced my coaches and headed straight to the warm-down pool. I remember sharing that time with Vic by my side at the warm-down pool. We had gone through so much together. I think we both felt shocked and relieved.

"After she made the 400 IM, I was able to walk around as coach with her, and that was a special moment," Vic said.

One day of the trials down and she was an Olympian again. Her week wasn't over, however, not by a long shot. The pressure was off, and this underdog was ready to be unleashed. She won the 400 freestyle, then took second in the 200 butterfly. But perhaps the most exciting part was finishing third in the 200 freestyle. That didn't allow her to make the team in that event, but it qualified her for the 800 freestyle relay. For someone who swims the distance freestyle and longer stroke events, relays are usually out of reach. The sprint freestyle relay is for the sprinters, the medley relay is for the fastest sprinters in each stroke, and the 800 freestyle relay is for those who can put together a 200. Occasionally, a distance specialist will break into that group, putting together a fast 200 freestyle and earning a spot on the Olympic relay team. That was what Kaitlin accomplished. She qualified for the Olympic team in three individual events and her first relay. She was all set up for a memorable time in Athens.

"Schubert was really happy for me but also reminded me I still had many more days of racing. I wasn't going to swim the 400 free originally, but he told me to swim it for prelims to help swim off the 400 IM," Kaitlin said.

Kaitlin representing Team USA at the 2003 Duel in the Pool in Indianapolis.
Peter H. Bick

I ended up having a great prelims swim that seeded me first for finals. I was not expecting that! So we figured I had better race it in finals. I had a great race, going a best time and actually winning the event. I felt so strong and awesome that race. I really felt in control from start to finish. I was so shocked by the whole thing. I was at ease after the 400 IM because I knew I had made the team, and I had no expectations for that 400 free. I just listened to Schubert and swam it! Pinch me, did that just happen? I was on a roll.

And there were plenty of other events yet to go.

The 200 IM, 200 free, and 200 fly all overlapped, so I always needed to pick two out of the three. The 200 free was like a sprint to me. Schubert instilled the confidence in me that I could swim it well enough to make the relay team [top six]. I had never been on a relay team. You don't swim on a relay for the 400 IM.

Kaitlin preparing to represent Team USA. *Peter H. Bick*

I didn't have enough confidence in my breaststroke to swim the 200 IM because Natalie [Coughlin] was swimming it and Amanda [Beard] was swimming it and Katie Hoff was swimming it. It was so stacked. I ended up swimming the 200 fly and 200 free. There was a semi and final overlap somewhere. I ended up getting third in the 200 free, and I was completely blown away that I made the relay team. Got to semis in the 200 fly. Then ended up second to Dana Kirk. Not only did I make the team, I made it in three individuals and a relay. It was surreal, a trials meet I couldn't even have imagined. Not only did I qualify to swim at trials, but I had made it on the 2004 Olympic team in not one, two, three but four events. Pinch me [again!], did that just happen?!

And it can't be overstated that this all happened so close to home, with her entire family there to watch every second of Kaitlin's triumph. "That was amazing, being in so close to my hometown," she said.

I love Long Beach. My mom is from Long Beach. It kind of came full circle. All of our championship meets were in Long Beach, and I had never had a bad meet there. Even when I wasn't swimming well at Michigan and came to a Grand Prix meet here, I swam well. I came back from a meet in Mexico sick and still swam well there.

The family atmosphere was tough to beat for Kaitlin and the rest of the Sandeno clan.

"For me being the one not as involved, Long Beach trials was really special for me," sister Amy said.

I was just so proud of her. It was an incredible experience. We always felt this enormous pride. Watching my parents get her to and from swimming for all of those years. Swimming was just something Kaitlin did. We believed she totally had a gift. It took up a lot of their time, but she still lived a normal life. There was a lot of focus on it, but it didn't take away from anything as a whole. My parents said she was going to go to school events, and stuff like that brought a lot of normalcy. I knew it was a huge deal that my sister went to the Olympics, but that is just what she did. She was a swimmer. It was such a gift. I have kids that are swimming and in other sports, and you see some of these parents and it is crazytown. It has trickled down to how I raise my kids and keep them well rounded.

While Kaitlin's stellar performance in the pool is well documented and well remembered, it was what she did out of the water that week that stuck with her roommate, Diana Munz. "That was a really hard meet for me to be honest. To me, she was there for me as a friend that entire meet," Diana said.

The first race was the 400 free for me, and I got ninth in prelims, barely made finals, and ended up third. My next race, same ordeal. I got 16th in the 200 free, missed the finals. I mean, these were races that I medaled in during the 2000 Olympics. So my last race was the 800. She was by my side the entire time. I remember swimming it and her diving over the lane lines to hug me. We were so excited that we were going together again. We made it.

Those were the kinds of meets where you needed a friend like that. There are so many times in swimming where you have down times instead of the great ones. When you have a friend that can carry you over the line and be there for you, it makes all the difference. I mean everybody has been there at some point of their career. I remember the moment of me being just completely exhausted and being so relieved that I made the team. She was there, just bringing her energy, and brought me to the highest level. That was awesome. I definitely thought I was prepared by all means. I had trained well. I went into it wanting to just do the same thing that I did in Sydney, and do better.

I had become a professional at that point, and I think there were a lot of ex-pectations I had from others. Going into it in 2000 was different because I was a kid with no expectations. Four years later was much different. Now I am working for my career. There was a lot of pressure, but I was trying not to think that way. Kaitlin and I took a step back and realized we love to swim. That is why we were in the sport in the first place. That is something my family and Kaitlin's family helped with a ton. We had to remember to go out and do something because we wanted to do it, not because someone else wanted us to do it.

Sandeno's performance was so dominant that after the trials, she was of-fered a contract by several sponsors. To sign, she would have to give up her senior year of eligibility at USC. It is a tough decision for any swimmer, espe-cially one who loves being part of a college team. Kaitlin was a captain of the team but at the same time had accomplished just about everything she wanted to in a college pool. Meanwhile, this would be huge exposure going into the Olympics and something that would allow her to be financially stable enough to swim professionally.

"I ended up signing like a day after that. That was hard. It was one of the hardest phone calls I have ever made, telling Schubert I was giving up my senior year of eligibility," she said. "I never thought I would do that."

Part of what made this opportunity so special is because she signed with Nike. A lot of swimmers in her situation signed with Speedo, which signed a larger group of swimmers each year. Nike was different. In fact, it was an even rarer opportunity than Kaitlin realized, since Nike would only sponsor elite swimmers for a few years.

I signed with Nike, a four-and-a-half-year contract. It had a base salary and also financial incentives [for doing well in the pool]. My teammates were supportive. It was an opportunity that really didn't exist, especially for females. Speedo kind of signed everybody big, but Nike signed a couple and I was their fifth. I knew the opportunity would never again arise like that. The timing was everything. Before the trials, I thought I would be done swimming after senior year. I had this amazing trials and felt good, and finally loved swimming again. I was never a person afraid to swim against anybody. I had some great meets to get that fire back. It was a 4.5-year contract. I knew that was never going to exist again. I signed for whatever it was, then there were bonuses for how I did at the Olympics, but I had a great Olympics, so that was nice.

Of course, that meant the end of swimming for USC. "It was a bummer, just from the college standpoint," USC coach Mark Schubert said.

But we talked, and she made it pretty evident that it was a deal of a lifetime. Nike was just breaking into the swimsuit market, and the people they signed did really well. You can't argue with that. But, of course, you would like her to be able to finish her college career. I just felt blessed to have that opportunity to coach her, then we went onto the Olympics—and it was fabulous.

It was a relationship that lasted as long as Nike did swimwear in the professional sense. "They treated me amazing. My dad was adamant that part of the contract was they would have to finish paying for my education. Still to this day I have reaped the benefits of that contract because of savings," Kaitlin said.

"Getting her degree after taking some time off from school. That was very important to me," Tom said. Kaitlin graduated from USC with a degree in social sciences with an emphasis in history in 2006.

Once she was a professional, other offers started to roll in.

Kaitlin added, "Then I signed with Mutual of Omaha [and other contracts], then appearances, and at that time clinics paid a lot of money. I mean it is nothing like professional football or baseball contracts, but it was comfortable living."

After making the team in four events, including her first relay, then turning professional with a lucrative contract, things couldn't have looked any better for Sandeno. She had again proved to be one of the nation's best swimmers and definitely the most versatile female swimmer. Teammates knew it. Opponents knew it. Fans saw it, and now sponsors saw it. It was a lot of pressure in a short amount of time. Kaitlin was eager to prove to everyone that she could do the same on the world's stage—challenge accepted.

8

GOLDEN IN GREECE

In one of the more perfect scenarios, Kaitlin Sandeno had turned in one of the strongest Olympic trials performances in women's swimming history—and she did it in what could only be described as her backyard pool.

After her stunning performance in Long Beach, California, the stage that was a little more than 20 minutes from home—like seemingly everything else Kaitlin was ready to prove she could be as successful in Greek pools as she was in California pools.

Kaitlin had proven a lot in her career already, but qualifying for four events in the 2004 Athens Olympic Games proved even more. She was not a one-Olympic wonder, a teen phenom who faded out. She was again going to be one of the faces of the Olympics, this time for different reasons. In 2000, Kaitlin was a smiling, bubbly teenager—full of personality—and she had captivated the nation as an Olympian. Four years later, while Michael Phelps was aiming for history, Kaitlin was out to prove that women could be just as versatile in the water and that she could swim faster than ever before—maybe even see a 400 IM time that wasn't 4:40.

Her Olympic program would include the 400 IM, 400 freestyle, 200 butterfly, and 800 freestyle relay. It was unlike any Olympic program seen before in swimming, especially women's swimming. Even Phelps wasn't racing two 400-meter races in back-to-back nights—and he didn't in 2008 either, when he won a record-breaking eight gold medals in Beijing.

That wasn't intimidating to Kaitlin, who was accustomed to a unique variety of events. In fact, the loaded schedule would bring out the best in the versatile champion, starting with her very first event.

As in 2000, the 400 IM was on the first night of the Olympics. Sandeno was used to missing the opening ceremonies and being the first in the water. She was also used to facing Yana Klochkova, of Ukraine, in the event. Yana was the gold medalist in 2000, beating Kaitlin head-to-head in Sydney, and the favorite to repeat in Athens.

Kaitlin knew what it would take to beat Yana. She would have to elevate her performance in the breaststroke leg of the race and exceed her usual speed in the other strokes as well. It was a tall order, but putting a complete race together would give Kaitlin a chance to knock off Yana and maybe even finally see a time faster than 4:40 on the scoreboard.

As she prepared for this showdown in the weeks between trials and the Olympics, Kaitlin was focused on her breaststroke. She picked the brains of coaches, teammates, anyone who could give her a little insight. Her maturity and ability to ask others for guidance was what separated her from a teenage Olympic rookie. She was a seasoned veteran looking to be herself and ready to do everything she could to earn a gold medal.

"My body kind of slendered that year from eating well and training. I felt like my body was adapting for success. I was just extremely happy to be there. One of the Team USA coaches, Eddie Reese, told me in the middle of the meet that I looked like a different swimmer. Happier," Kaitlin said.

> I am typically a happy, upbeat person. I felt the pride putting the American cap on. I couldn't believe I got to do this again. Then what I learned from 2000 carried over. I was just going for best times. Honestly my only actual goal was to break 4:40. I knew what I needed to do for the 400 IM. I knew it was in the breaststroke, and I put it on myself to focus on that. I stress that whenever I do speaking engagements, because it is ultimately on you. Your coach can tell you what to do, but you have to do it. I would ask world record holder Brendan Hansen for insight, I asked other coaches and specialists to look at my breaststroke. I know it was there somewhere because at one point, I was a breaststroker. That was my focus. At training camp, I had some shoulder is-sues, but I just switched to kick sets when that happened and pushed myself as hard as I could in those.

Kaitlin roomed with Diana Munz for the second consecutive Olympic Games, and the two veterans made a new friend in Olympic rookie Ryan Lochte.

"I roomed again with Diana Munz, and that was pure joy," Kaitlin said. "We were close with Ryan Lochte. We were three super upbeat peas in a pod. Being older and having gone through it, I wanted to take it in. I took that for granted in 2000."

So Kaitlin had that mind-set when she stepped onto the blocks for her first race, the preliminaries of the 400 individual medley. Whatever seriousness she tried to bring to the race was gone the second she looked at the clock.

"The morning of the 400 IM prelims, I went 4:40 again," she said. "It was laughable. I started laughing."

It was fast enough to make the finals and set her up in a lane next to top seed Yana Klochkova. Team USA coach Mark Schubert said watching Kaitlin swim the 400 IM was one of his favorite moments in coaching—especially after all of the injuries she had overcome at USC leading up to Athens.

"She was so fun to coach because she was so good in all four strokes. It never got boring," he said.

I was convinced it would work out, and I just had to help her stick with it. Even at training camp before Athens, she was struggling with a shoulder problem, and she had to kick most of training camp. She was phenomenal in the sets that she would do. She would put some fins on and keep up with the guys swimming when she was just kicking. Sometimes I wonder if that situation didn't help her because it gave her enough rest. Oftentimes I wondered if I gave her enough rest on her taper. She did then and had the meet of her life.

Sandeno cooled down after her preliminary race and went back to her room to begin her prefinals routine.

I was pretty informal. I was never really that nervous. I used to stretch a lot. I don't know if that was listening to my body or trying to handle my nerves. I was pretty chatty. I would always eat a banana after warm-ups. As I got older, I liked to incorporate coffee on my way to the pool. I was pretty laid back in general. I liked to be one of the last people up on the blocks. That was kind of my thing.

Only this time, things were a little different. Excitement had taken over.

"I was so excited to race that night that I couldn't sleep," she said.

I usually take a nap. I felt extra pressure and pride because Katie Hoff didn't qualify for finals, so it was just me for Team USA. My soccer coaches used to make sure I was in the shootout because they said I had ice in my veins, and it reminded me of that. I can handle this pressure. I want this kind of pressure.

It was a mentality that elevated her maturity. Kaitlin was four years and thousands of miles from Sydney when she was intimidated by Klochkova. After all, what teenager wouldn't be a little intimidated? Four years later, it was a different story. Sandeno was not intimidated, she was excited. But she was still facing the best in the world. This time, she didn't seem as unbeatable, however.

"I had a joyful smile, not a nervous smile this time. I get up to the blocks and who am I next to? Yana Klochkova. Again. This is four years ago all over again," Sandeno said.

> But I knew not to swim her race. I took it out smooth and easy. I was third after the fly and got to the backstroke and I had really great underwaters, and most foreign swimmers did not have good underwaters at that time, and I kind of pulled myself up to second just with my underwater kickout. I had a really nice backstroke leg. Getting to the breaststroke, I was right behind Yana.

Now, all of the work, all of the questions, and all of the dedication to breast-stroke training, the moment of truth was here for Kaitlin. It was time to prove she had four elite strokes.

"I could see myself pulling up to Yana in the breaststroke," Kaitlin said.

> I felt strong, and I was getting more excited. Later, when I was swimming for Bob Bowman, I heard him describe an out-of-body-experience race. That is the one and only time I had ever felt like that. Not tired, no fatigue, just felt so good and so in control. We were basically tied when we touched for the freestyle.

Just 100 meters to go, and the excitement was building. This wasn't Yana pulling away, as she had done four years earlier. Kaitlin and Yana were locked in one of the most epic duels in swimming history. It was going to come down to who could finish better.

"The last turn, I came up before her, and the team was going crazy. We were literally stroke for stroke," Kaitlin remembered.

> I looked up when I touched and I saw "Sandeno, USA, 2." I was like okay, silver. Then I got this huge smile on my face. I remember looking at my block to make sure I was looking at the right lane. And it said 4:34.95, and I lost it. I could not believe it. I was jumping up and down and celebrating. People were looking at me like, "You didn't win." But I couldn't believe that happened: 4:34 was my gold medal.

Jon Urbanchek saw something different in Sandeno that race. It was the start of a dominating Olympic Games. "She was on fire," he said.

> Her time for the last 100 freestyle was like a 1:01. In those days, that was almost unheard of. She just ran everybody down at the end. It was really close. If they

had to go two more meters, she would have won. She had a lot of confidence. She is a racer. She loves to race. It doesn't matter what it is. In training camp, we played some soccer, and she was playing with the boys and scoring on all of them. She is what we really needed in swimming, an athletic woman.

Kaitlin and her coaches weren't the only ones going crazy. Family, friends, and Team USA fans in the stands—and people watching throughout the world—were excited about the first U.S. medal of the Games.

"I remember looking up, and Diana and Ryan were just going nuts," Kaitlin said. "I thought they were going to fall out of the bleachers. I was trying to find my parents in the sea of people."

Her parents were overjoyed. "She was stuck on that time for so long. She was just so happy, and there was no pressure," Tom Sandeno said. "That was so exciting."

It immediately rubbed off on her teammates as they were preparing for the biggest swims of their careers. "Her time drop in the 400 IM was insane," Natalie Coughlin said. "I am sure that everyone in the stands and teammates that weren't racing that night, it pumped them up for the week. Swims like that get everyone fired up, and you want to build upon what Team USA is doing."

It even fired up past swimming legends, who took pride in the way Kaitlin's energy jump-started a memorable Olympics for Team USA.

"Kaitlin is one of those swimmers that you hope for on a national team. You want somebody with personality that shines through the moment they walk in. It is endless energy. It is a positive force the moment she smiles—which happens all the time," Olympic gold medalist Summer Sanders said.

> A lot of her teammates needed that. I love the fact that she had the guts to do the 400 IM, which is one of the most brutal events. Any time I see an American doing well and showing grit in that 400 IM, I am proud. It helps that she is a vivacious personality as well. Swimmers are in the water with cap and goggles on. You have those personalities, and you remember them. They are not just these robots that follow the black line at the bottom of the pool back and forth.

Then it was time to face the reporters, one of the toughest things to do when a race doesn't go well. But this was one of the easiest interviews of her career.

"You go through the media as soon as you exit the pool, and the first question I got was along the lines of, 'You were this close to winning gold, how does that feel?' That time was my gold," Kaitlin commented. "Four years—and a crappy four years of swimming if we are being honest. That was my gold. And I am in no way upset to be receiving a silver medal around my neck."

"That is her talk now, the idea that her silver was her gold," Bree Deters said.

We were all so excited. The 400 IM, her time. She didn't just break her best time, she blew it away. I remember hearing the commentators talk about her getting so close to gold and not winning. I was like, "Do they even know her at all?" I was almost angry to hear everyone put that spin on it, that she only won silver. How many people ever get to compete at that level, let alone win a medal at the Olympics? Blowing her own expectations out of the water every step of the way in 2004. That was really cool to watch.

Especially after receiving the versatile training Vic and Renee Riggs ensured each one of their swimmers mastered. "It is 100 percent from the training program we came from," Deters said.

It was a distance-based program, but our coaches carried the versatility and endurance. We did a lot of yardage, but we always all trained IM. We were always doing IM sets and freestyle sets. We were encouraged—and forced, I suppose—to compete in everything. I was a terrible breaststroker, but at least once or twice a season I had to swim it in a meet. They made all of us do that. They wanted us to have the ability to race all of the events.

Kaitlin proved she could do that, but with her time drop in the 400 IM, she had proven even more. "Well to go from 4:40, which she had done about 10 or 12 times—and she was so frustrated with it—to go 4:34 was just unreal," Mark Schubert said.

It is unreal for a swimmer that caliber to drop that much at the Olympics Games. The thing that I remember the most is after the swim, I was waiting for her at the warm-up pool. She came out of the interview area and had the biggest smile I have ever seen. She was overjoyed. It was kind of ironic because she lost the race by like a 10th of a second. She was so proud of herself. I was so happy about that. Somebody without that same perspective wouldn't have felt that way.

But her teammates knew how important breaking 4:40 was to her. It was something that had taken a long time to break—a long time.
"She totally dominated," Diana said.

With swimming, I swear when you start off a meet that good, you know you are just going to rock it for the rest of the meet. Your confidence level is so high, you are at the highest level possible, and you have so much support around you. As soon as she swam that race—and it wasn't even about her getting the silver medal, it was about her conquering something that she had been trying to conquer time-wise for so long—you just knew the light in her had an extra oomph in it. It took her really far. It was fun to experience it with her and see all of the amazing things that she had going forward for her. That was just the start. That is the first day. It totally jump-started the entire team.

But being a distance swimmer, you can go years plateauing at a number that you just can't shake. It is hilarious talking to younger kids these days who are stressing that they haven't gotten a best time in months. Every distance swimmer has a plateau that was so solid that you never think you are going to break it. But when you do break it, you break it so hard that you have a moment like that. Her timing was impeccable. She just totally nailed it.

It was a defining moment in Kaitlin's career, but her week was just beginning. She had three more events on her schedule, including the 400 freestyle the following day. After talking to reporters, she had a lot to do that night and had to try to get some rest before another race.

"I needed to go warm down. Coach Schubert told me the next day would be the hardest," Kaitlin reflected.

I finally got to see my parents between the fences. Then I had to do urine and blood drug testing. I had to do urine at the pool, then go back to the village and do blood testing. I had to sit there and watch them test it. I swear it was like 2:30 a.m. when I got back to my room. It was nuts. Klete Keller had won a bronze in the 400 free, and we were on the same agenda heading back to the village, so he and I were zombies. Happy zombies . . . not like I was going to sleep a wink anyway. I slept two hours, and the 400 free hurt so bad. I think I was sixth going into finals.

Not that she was complaining. Not everyone gets to be a "happy zombie."

"The 400 free prelims was the hardest. I was scared I wasn't going to make it into finals, but I did in sixth. Again, our other American didn't make it so it was going to be me," Kaitlin said. "I remember going back to my room to try to sleep, but I was wide awake before the final."

There was a lot to think about. She was still basking in her American-record performance in the 400 IM but had to think about her race strategy for the 400 freestyle—and hope she had enough in the tank to execute it.

"I like to negative split [swimming faster as the event goes on], so I was picking them off as I went, seventh, sixth, fifth," she said, recalling how she passed several competitors in the final 150 meters. "The 400 free was my biggest shocker because I didn't even think I was going to swim it at trials. So when I looked up and saw third, I was blown away. It was a great time [4:06.19], and I medaled."

Two-for-two with two to go. It was a lot to process. Thankfully, Kaitlin had a day without a race following her bronze medal performance. She didn't have to compete, but it was far from relaxing. "The next day was an off day for me, and I got to do the *Today Show* and *Access Hollywood*. I had such a blast being on those shows. It was cool to experience the hype that you get afterward," she said.

Kaitlin was now one of the early stars of the Athens Games, but one thing was still eluding her: a gold medal. After a busy off day, she would have two chances with the 200 butterfly and the 800 freestyle relay.

"In the relay, I was going to have to swim prelims and kind of prove myself to see if I would swim in finals. But probably one of the coolest, most selfless acts would allow me to rest during the prelim relay," Kaitlin continued.

> Lindsay Benko was our captain and someone I swam with at USC, and always someone I looked up to. She felt like she was swimming off, so she told the coaches that she should have to swim in the prelims to earn her spot in finals, so they kept me out of prelims because they knew I was swimming well and I had the 200 fly that day.

It wasn't the ideal situation for Benko, but it was something she felt she had to do for her team. She had led the United States to the gold medal in that same relay four years prior—when she and Kaitlin were also teammates—and was not about to get in the way of another gold medal performance by her country.

"In Athens, Kaitlin gave me so much support when I wasn't having the meet I wanted to have. And she was having a stellar meet. For her to reach out and support me in a way that she did when she was having the meet of her life was incredible," Benko said. "It was a totally different dynamic the second time around. I think we take it for granted that very few people get to make two. While I didn't have the greatest meet in Athens, I certainly appreciated it a lot more."

And she appreciated the opportunity her team had in the relay, something that is still talked about as one of the biggest moments in U.S. swimming history.

"I tried to pave the way for her to be on the podium, and I think that is very special to know that she and others appreciated that," Benko said.

> I volunteered to swim in the morning. I knew I wasn't having the meet that I wanted to have, so instead of making that a coach's decision, which I know can be extremely difficult, I wasn't going to help the team the way others could. I said I would be willing to swim the morning. I don't know if that decision made it easier on anybody or harder on anybody, but it was something I felt was the right thing to do for the team.

Benko watched Kaitlin anchor one of the defining swims of her career and one of the biggest moments for the U.S. women in Olympic history.

"It is so cool so see someone you know have a meet like that. It is hard to let your disappointment get in the way of knowing how hard she has worked. It was really fun to watch her," Benko said.

> It was pretty difficult to watch, to be honest, but special at the same time. You are watching teammates doing something extremely special.
>
> Now that it is so far removed, it was extremely painful at the time, but extremely exciting at the time. Now it is just exciting. Her enthusiasm definitely helps. When you see something like that [her dropping six seconds in the 400 IM to kick off the meet], you feel like something special is about to happen. You see that as teammates and feel like if she can do that, we can do something like that. It definitely helps the team. It was pure joy when she touched.

That gesture took a lot of pressure off of Kaitlin, who had to balance her focus between a relay and an individual event in the same day.

"I felt really good in the fly, but after semifinals, I was seeded first and I was shocked. I wasn't used to that, and I didn't like that. I like being in an outside lane and chasing, not being chased," Sandeno said.

> I think I put more pressure on myself being seeded first. That got in my head a little bit. Eddie Reese said I was acting different before that race than any other race. I ended up fourth, but it was a best time, so I couldn't hang my head. The recovery time was really quick for the relay. I think Schubert almost likes when I don't swim well because he knows my next race is going to be great. He just told me to get ready for that relay. I went to the warm-down pool and got my head ready.

Swimming mostly the 400 IM and longer-distance races, it would be Sandeno's first—and only—relay experience at the Olympics. It would be one of the biggest relays in the history of the sport.

Sandeno continued,

> Walking out for the relay was incredible. I had never been on an international relay before, let alone at the Olympics. They were like, "Kaitlin, we are just going to put you on the finals relay," and I was like, "Whoa." Then they told me I was going to anchor. . . . "Whoa! Oh okay!" I was kind of blown away by that and honored by that. We walked out and had our little group relay meeting. Natalie Coughlin was the leadoff and basically forewarned us not to be nervous if she's not leading after the first 100, she was going for a negative split. I went and sat on the floor with my back up against the wall of the bleachers. I was just trying to

get my mind right and make sure the 200 fly was out of me. Plus I wanted to rest
my legs because I still had a 600 of waiting ahead of me. Natalie did just what she
said. She was definitely not in first after the 100. We were the favorite, and Natalie
kicked it into a high gear and got us the lead. Carly Piper maintained that lead,
and Dana Vollmer increased it.

Now, it was Kaitlin's time to put her mark in the record books and grab the
gold. The United States had a sizeable lead going into Kaitlin's anchor leg. It
was within her grasp. All she had to do was take it.

"I got on the blocks and was thinking the gold medal was on the silver platter
right now. We were that far ahead. The world record was never in my head. I
have never been that swimmer that knows what the record is or how close I am
to a record," she added.

I never knew my times growing up. The biggest thing going through my mind
was to not false start the relay. So I joke that I had the slowest relay exchange in
Olympic history because she literally touched the wall, then I circled my arms
and dove in. I remember having to control my excitement in the first 100. The
Chinese were creeping up a little bit on Carly, so I knew someone else was going
to be within striking distance. I remember pushing off the wall for the last 100 and
letting it rip. It was my last Olympic swim.

Only she didn't know it at the time. She just knew that everyone in the arena
was going crazy like something extra special was in the works.

Coming home, I saw the side of the pool and everyone standing up. It didn't really register what that meant, but watching it on TV later, they started to stand
up with that world record yellow line on the screen. As I was coming home, I remember thinking I have a silver medal, then a bronze medal, and now I am going
to get a gold medal. It was like, "Oh my gosh this is really happening right now!"
Coming into the flags, when I touched, I was screaming as I finished. I looked up
at the wall and saw the scoreboard and it said USA, 1, WR. I had to ask Natalie if
it was really a world record, and she was like, "Yes, it is a world record!"

I had no idea what the record was, and everyone went ballistic. It felt like
other countries definitely respected what we had just done, breaking the oldest
record in the history books, the last East German record. The Australians came
right over and shook our hands. That pure excitement of what we had just accomplished was pretty surreal. For the first time, being on the top podium with
the flag going up, and you are standing with your team and hearing the national
anthem. Chills just go down your spine. It is a mix of an emotion between tears
and giggling. You are trying to find your family in the crowd. You are trying to

stay in the moment, sharing this with three other girls. It was a whirlwind. But the flag goes up, and chills go through your body.

And after an entire career spent competing against Coughlin, there they were, side by side as teammates in one of the most memorable women's swimming moments in Olympic history.

"I definitely feel closer to Natalie now than I did when we were racing. I always really respected her. She was so talented," Kaitlin reflected.

That relay is always something I will be proud of. Natalie has that laser-beam focus. She took it easy the first 100, and I was getting nervous, but crushed the back half and put us into the lead. I was so happy to have that memory with Natalie. It is a really special moment we share. I recently shared a picture of our relay on social media and she commented, "#BestAnchorEver," in which I responded, "#BestLeadOffEver." It has been neat reconnecting with her. I feel like I have gotten to know her more than just as swimmers, as women, as wives, and just what is going on in our lives.

Kaitlin and Natalie Coughlin have been around one another on the pool deck for decades as competitors, Olympic teammates, and friends. *Sandeno collection*

Coach Schubert was there to see the East German record, then finally see that record fall. "I was at the Olympics in 1976, when the women got skunked, and was coaching Shirley Babashoff. To see them break that East German record, that was such a dirty record, was a huge thrill," Schubert said.

> Relays are selected not only from results of the trials, but based on coaches' observations of who is swimming well at the meet. It was pretty much the consensus of the coaches to put her on the relay. I was the head coach, but they all agreed we wanted her on the relay. Anchoring it was my choice. I was prejudiced and confident. When somebody drops the way she did at that meet, it is not rocket science that she is going to swim that well. When things are going your way, they are going your way.

The relay was one of the defining moments for Coughlin, Piper, and Vollmer as well. "I have never been on a national team relay knowing we were going to win, but we had so much confidence that we were going to destroy the field. I had never been on a relay like that before, nor have I since. That was an incredible feeling. The whole relay was kind of a celebration," Coughlin said.

> Kaitlin was really on fire that meet. She was just hot. Coach Schubert made the right call putting her on that relay. I led off, Carly Piper and Dana Vollmer were the middle two legs. Kaitlin was the anchor. By that point, she was so far ahead, it was like, "Oh my God, we are going to break this record." It was the last East German world record, so that gold medal celebration was such a celebration. We were so joyous and really singing the national anthem. It was really special to be on that top podium with those three other girls.

It was a special performance because, while Michael Phelps was aiming for history and winning six gold medals, Natalie and Kaitlin together became the faces of the 2004 Olympics for the women. They each had stellar performances and joined forces for the biggest race of the meet.

"Kaitlin was just on fire. Kind of like Maya DiRado in the last Olympics [2016]. She had the biggest meet of her life at the most important time," Coughlin said. "Kaitlin was really hot when it mattered, and every performance built on the previous one. She just had so much momentum. It was really special to see."

Jon Urbanchek was one of the coaches going crazy during the relay. "Athens was awesome. For Kaitlin, that was the first time she got the gold medal, plus silver in the 400 IM. It was a great experience for her," he said.

On the other side of the world, the excitement was spreading throughout the United States, especially among those closest to Kaitlin.

"Athens was her shining moment," Vic Riggs said.

That was obviously the meet you dream about for a kid. It was like . . . thank God. We knew it was there. She knew it was there. The pieces had never fallen together. I don't know why they did that night, but her competition was a little bit of a motivating factor. There are those out-of-body experiences. I had three of them when I raced. I went 15:00 in the 1,650, and I don't remember most of that. You hit a level that you can't really explain it. She was like, "This isn't going to happen again. It is going to take an incredible swim to medal, and I am going to do it." It was mixed emotions because Lindsay gave her spot up after having not a great meet. You know she is done, this is it for her. To hear that but then to see Kaitlin and the others do what they did, it is such an emotional high. You still hear arguments about the East Germans today. To have that last record be broken and be ours was amazing and emotional.

"At that point, she was family," Kammy Miller said.

It was unbelievably exciting seeing everything come together for her. She is a champion. That year really solidified that for her on the collegiate level and on the Olympic stage. Everything was gold. From a friendship perspective, being able to watch a friend achieve those accolades, know what those struggles have been, and achieve the highest level in the sport is an unbelievable thing to watch and be proud of.

"I remember watching from my college apartment," Amy Walloch said. "I remember the relay. I remember being so excited. Holy sh—! She just broke a world record and is a gold medalist!"

"Her second Olympics was after some extra drama and injuries surrounding her in college," Bree Deters said.

She was not in any of the drama but was captaining a team that had a lot of drama. There were a lot of ups and downs. I'm sure there were questions in her mind about what 2004 was going to bring. It was emotional for me watching her succeed after all of that. She was a good freestyler, but to see her anchoring that relay—I was just so proud of her.

It all happened in a blur. And it took days and even years to put the race into a proper historical perspective.

"I don't even think we realized in that moment how big of a deal that was," Kaitlin said.

I didn't realize until 2016, when I interviewed the women from the *Last Gold* documentary at Olympic trials, and seeing everything they went through with the

East Germans. It made it hit home a little more. Now that I am older and have gotten to experience that a little more, it is really surreal.

Kaitlin wanted to soak in the moment, and she did so with Diana attached at the hip, as always. After they finished their meet, they soaked in the energy in Athens and enjoyed being in the limelight with a little Mediterranean nightlife.

"We were coming home, our last night in Athens. We went to a really awesome party. Commuting around was really tough. Our bus was leaving at a certain time to get us to the airport," Kaitlin said.

We were running through the village so late because we had to go and we hadn't packed. Stuff was literally everywhere in our room. We threw everything in suitcases. So we went from this awesome party, to running through the village, back to our room, and ran to the bus. Everybody just stared at us because they were waiting for us. I will never forget that. One time we had to run through the village again to get back for curfew. Diana's feet hurt really bad because she wore the worst shoes. Her feet hurt so bad. I had her on my back. I had to run through the village with her on my back. That is a teammate right there. And we didn't miss curfew. We did all of these afterparties. They were all sponsored by somebody. Amanda Beard was sponsored by Red Bull, so we went to Red Bull parties. There was an *Entertainment Tonight* party. We didn't do these things until our swimming was done. But there was always something to go to. But both Olympics, it was really hard to get from the athlete village to these places. In Sydney, we had to take a ferry at one point. There was definitely something to do every night.

The gold medal and world record had a lasting impact on Sandeno's career, which at the end of the 2004 Olympics was at its peak.

"I just love to race, and I finally felt like I was back. I didn't feel like I was myself for so long because of all of the things I had to go through," she said.

The physical things I had to overcome, but that definitely takes a toll on your mental side of things, too, which I feel like for me, my mental side is a big reason of why I was so good. I definitely had to overcome that with the injuries and the weight gain, wondering if I wanted to do this anymore.

But a legendary performance to close out the Athens Games erased those doubts. Sandeno was happy in the water and ready to continue her career.

I didn't know it at the time, but it was my last swim ever in the Olympics. I got a gold, silver, bronze, world record, American record, and a fourth—1-2-3-4, that is pretty cool. That was the first time in a long time that I was really happy swimming again. A lot of times you are happy because you swim well, but that Olympics I really swam well because I was happy. A fast swimmer is a happy swimmer, but sometimes it needs to be the other way around. At the trials, I was so dead set at improving my 400 IM best time. I wasn't even happy with that swim, even after I made the team. I was annoyed, but it was definitely motivating. I knew I wasn't breaking 4:40 if I didn't improve my breaststroke. You can't get better if you don't face your weaknesses. It is not fun to work on your weaknesses, but to be your best, you have to. I had not been enjoying swimming for quite some time leading up to the Olympics, but once I qualified, I was having so much fun. I put in some crazy hard work between trials and the Olympics, but I was having the time of my life. I was on cloud nine the entire time as soon as I made the team. I couldn't even sleep I was so excited.

Kaitlin had finally struck gold and experienced signature moments as part of a relay and individually. As epic as the relay performance was, the race she remembers most is the 400 IM duel she had with Yana.

"The 4:34 still stands out for me. It is my proudest race in my entire career," Kaitlin said.

I am more aware of the history of that record of the relay now, but being on a relay team is different experience. I never trained with Natalie, Carly, or Dana. We were thrown together because we were the four fastest Americans. It is different than your team winning a NCAA relay as you trained day in and day out together. Yes, we stood up there sharing national pride, and don't get me wrong, I am so proud of what we accomplished, but for me, the 400 IM was the most special. That was everything that I had overcome and had to deal with to get there. That was all on me—different than being on a relay. The gold medal and world record is a honor [and look really good on a resume and e-mail signature], but my 400 IM was my personal feat after everything. I got out of the pool and was wondering what this feeling was that I was feeling. It was the first time ever in my swimming career that I felt really, really proud of myself. My parents always told me I was too hard on myself over the years, and I don't think I ever realized in the moment what I had accomplished. But this was a new feeling as I swam to the side of the pool after my race. It really set the tone for the rest of my meet. I really had teammates and coaches say that race pumped up our team and set the tone for the entire meet. I was not supposed to be anywhere near Yana, and it was a really close race. She was considered unbeatable, and in the end it was the difference of 12 hundredths of a second.

That race put Kaitlin back in the ranks of the world's elite. She continued to prove that with every race she participated in while in Athens. In four very diverse events, she secured a gold, a silver, a bronze, and a fourth-place finish. It wasn't four golds, but it was four elite performances that proved to the world—and herself—that she was one of the most versatile and elite swimmers in Olympic history.

TRAINING FOR
THE TRIO

Now what? What does a swimmer do after going the fastest she has ever gone in her signature event, then anchoring a gold medal relay to cap off a spectacular Olympics?

It was complicated. Kaitlin Sandeno was now a professional swimmer, so she had no college team to return to, and after a second Olympics, she was again at another crossroads. Her contract with Nike wasn't finished, so a career as a professional swimmer was the plan; it was just a matter of details—the biggest being where to train.

In 2004, it wasn't like it is now, where there are many club choices for postcollege swimmers. Kaitlin only had a couple of options, but the one that made the most sense would cause her to move halfway across the country and challenge her desire to aim for a third Olympic team. Kaitlin decided to head to Ann Arbor, Michigan, to join the prestigious Club Wolverine. It wasn't an easy decision.

"Upon returning to the States after Athens, life was once again a post-Olympic whirlwind," she said.

Appearances, TV shows, photo shoots, sponsorship commitments, swim clinics, speeches, and, not to mention, I was still enrolled in classes at USC and had short-course world championships to prepare for in October. Just like in 2000, I needed a break from the pool, but having short-course world champs still kept me in the water a bit. The hardest part was trying to juggle all the traveling with my school commitment.

Something was going to have to give.

"I had a slight meltdown and wanted to drop out of school while talking to my mom on the phone," Kaitlin said. "She encouraged me to finish the semester but look into taking the following semester off. And that is exactly what I did. Boy did I need that! Life as a professional swimmer kept me busy. It was a challenge to stay diligent with my training while on the road so much."

"Coming back from the Olympics, everything was just in hyperdrive as far as turning pro and navigating those waters. Everything moved at lightning speed," Kammy Miller said.

I don't really remember talking with her about the possibility of going pro. I remember that finishing school was something very important to her and her parents. She did take a reprieve of school when she turned pro. I knew she was going to finish school. For her it made the most sense to go pro. I remember how exciting it was. We had a landline, and people would call the apartment and I would always answer the phone. She always joked that I should be her manager. You never knew who was calling. She used our little apartment as an office. It sounded far more glamorous than it was. We had a two-bedroom apartment and had a spiral staircase that went up to what we called the office. We each had a desk up there. From a friendship perspective, being able to watch a friend achieve those accolades, know what those struggles have been, and achieve the highest level in the sport is an unbelievable thing to watch and be proud of.

Miller got to be part of some of the limelight as well.

"I hadn't seen her since the Olympics. But I came back and drove her to her parents' house to spend the weekend there with them, which was not uncommon," Miller remembered.

We had just sat down at the kitchen table, and the phone rang. It was her agent asking if she wanted to present at the MTV Video Music Awards. She asked when it was, he said tomorrow. She asked where it was, he said it's in Miami. She said she was home, and he told her he was booking her on a red-eye tonight and she could bring a guest. She turns to me and says, "Wanna go to Miami tonight?" This is as we are sitting down to dinner. I was like, "Tonight? You mean, *tonight*, tonight?" We had just about zero time and nothing to wear. We ran to the mall, grabbed who knows what, and made some semblance of outfits. We took the red-eye. They flew us first class. We got picked up, and she was led to believe her hair and makeup would be all set when she got there. We get there and there is no hair, makeup, or wardrobe. I somehow managed to find someone to do her hair and makeup, and got a driver to pick us up. My friends call me MacGyver because I always figure things out like that.

We got to walk the red carpet. P-Diddy was there. It was 2004 and I am 20, she's 21. It was unbelievable. We are getting in there, and we were sitting behind Shaquille O'Neal. It seems like forever ago now. It was a cool, electric show that was just not normal. That was the first time it hit me that this is not how normal college students live. We had amazing seats, and she presented the final award with Kerri Walsh and Misty May and a couple other Olympians. The next morning, we found out we were being flown back on a private plane. I was 20, so I couldn't go to the afterparty, so Kaitlin didn't go either and we just went out to dinner and talked about it all. . . . "Pinch me . . . did that just happen?!" We took a bunch of selfies with disposable cameras. We were waiting for Misty May and Kerri Walsh on the private plane. They said there was one more person we were waiting for—it was Matthew Lillard. Then we were waiting for someone else . . . all of a sudden Dave Chappelle shows up. We all got on this tiny plane together. It was so fun. It was another one of those pinch me things. It is when it really started to sink in that things were different for Kaitlin. There were things like this and photo shoots and people wanting to see her medals. There was no two ways about it, she was famous. Watching her photo shoots for magazines was a really big deal. Watching her fame grow was really cool.

While basking in her Olympic success and balancing every aspect of her life, Kaitlin still had to keep training because the world championships, the biggest event in swimming outside of the Olympics, was just months away.

"Somehow I managed to pull off an incredible world champs," she said.

Looking back, it just might have been my most impressive meet. The event lineup was a doozy for me: 200 butterfly, 400 IM, and 800 free relay all on the same day, and then the 400 free a day after that! Not only did I win all three on the first day of the meet, but I did it with a slight concussion. I was involved in a warm-up collision that allowed me only a 75 [meters] of warm-up before getting knocked in the head, sending me to the trainer instead of finishing my premeet warm-up. This girl had a kickboard and did an aggressive touch and turn. Her kickboard went into my goggles and broke my goggles. I had just got in. I saw our team doctor and laid down. It wasn't a severe concussion, it was a slight one. The ball was in my court. I had three events that day. I think I was just going off of adrenaline. I didn't necessarily train a ton since I was coming off of an Olympic year. I was a gamer and a racer. I tended to step up in moments like that. I knew I wanted to suck it up and just race. Turned out to be one awesome night of racing. I followed that day up by winning the 400 free as well—4-for-4 at world champs and one of my most fun meets ever. There's nothing like competing at an international meet on home soil.

Following the world championships, things changed quickly at USC. It was just not the same not being on the college team. "Training at USC while not

Kaitlin during her days at Club Wolverine. *Peter H. Bick*

competing for the school was getting challenging. It was hard to be motivated, and my training routine needed to be much different than the college swimmers due to meet schedules," Kaitlin said.

> I was determined to get my degree as quick as I could and knew I needed a new training environment. At that time, there weren't many options for a place to go train for postcollege swimmers. And frankly, there weren't many programs that had postgrad women at them. Club Wolverine at University of Michigan seemed like the best program for my events. But this was an all-male team. After meeting with coach Bob Bowman and being in Ann Arbor a few times, I decided to give it a go.

It couldn't have been a more different environment. A club team with mostly men, a coach with a different approach, and a state with an actual winter. Kaitlin was in for the most challenging move of her life. Thankfully, she was reunited with coach Jon Urbanchek.

"The best thing at Club Wolverine was swimming for Urbanchek for two and a half years. He got me through the tough times. He was my shining light there," Sandeno commented.

> From sunny Southern California to cold, snowy Michigan, was I in for a shock. The day my mom dropped me off at the airport with a one-way ticket to Michigan was one of the hardest and saddest days of my life. I had never been so far from my family for an extended period of time. But part of me was excited. Something new, something outside of my normal, new chapter, a team full of incredibly strong swimmers, and not to mention so happy to be reunited with one of my closest friends and fellow Trojan teammates, Erik Vendt. I continued to press on but knew that 2008 would be my last year competing. Let it be trials or the Olympics, hopefully the Olympics. The goal was three Olympic teams.

Urbanchek saw Sandeno's arrival in Ann Arbor as a turning point for the Club Wolverine elite group, having a female of her caliber choose to come and train there. Most of the elite females they had trained were Michigan natives like Allison Schmitt and Kara Lynn Joyce.

"I retired in 2004 from Michigan right after Athens. Bob Bowman wanted me to stay with Club Wolverine so we could prepare for the next Olympics together," Urbanchek said.

> Club Wolverine became an elite preparation center for Beijing. We had so many great swimmers. We already had some great swimmers. We had Michael Phelps and Allison Schmitt, who was local. Eric Vendt and Klete Keller, who I recruited, ended up going to USC. The Vanderkaay brothers, Chris DeJong, Davis Tarwater, Chris Thompson. An unbelievable amount of athletes came to the group. Kaitlin came along—this was awesome because the environment was that of an Olympic culture. We all believed that we all were going to make the Olympics.

Kaitlin's training style was something Urbanchek was familiar with, but the other swimmers were able to see what her USC teammates had—that Kaitlin, while smiley and bubbly out of the water, gets down to business in the water.

"Kaitlin trained very hard," Urbanchek said.

> In 2006, I took a group of people to Europe for a tour that was in preparation for the national championships. We had a training session with hardcore training—30 times 50-meter butterfly from the dive with short rest. Somewhere at the end Kaitlin got to the point where she was literally bawling because she was so

tired. But she made it. I took the team to Europe like a week later. Kaitlin swam quite well in those three meets. In Barcelona, she swam the 200 fly, she did her lifetime best, faster than she went at the Olympics. I was able to use that moment. I told her a week ago, she was ready to quit. Ten days later, her lifetime best. I told her those 30 50s did it. You keep going until you go to the trash can and puke or something. Our training was hard core. You don't get out of training when it gets too hard and you are in tears. If it doesn't kill you it will help you.

Urbanchek saw how special Kaitlin was to the sport. It wasn't just her training, either. He continued,

When she came to Ann Arbor to train, Club Wolverine had about 200 kids in the program. We had the age group awards banquet, and Kaitlin was the keynote speaker to the group. Her mom ended up coming to that. Kaitlin got up to talk, and she introduced her mom. She said, "My mom is clueless about swimming, she doesn't know my times. We never talk about that kind of stuff. She always wanted to have the coach do the coaching. But one thing she always cared about [besides me being nice and happy] is having my cap, goggles, and suit match." If you look at her even today, that is what she still does. She always matches. She could be a swimming model.

Definitely a swimming role model. That was on display during the Toyota Southern California Grand Prix of Swimming in Long Beach in July 2007, after

Kaitlin swimming at the 2006 U.S. Open. *Peter H. Bick*

winning the 500 freestyle in 4:42.13. Shortly after Kaitlin touched the wall, a fellow competitor, Courtney Eads, of Upland, had to be pulled out of the pool by lifeguards. Kaitlin immediately rushed over to help. Courtney started having physical problems near the end of the race, what her coach believed was a seizure, according to a January 14, 2007, *Los Angeles Times* article. After Eads was pulled out of the water, Kaitlin helped by taking deep breaths with her in tandem. "By the way she couldn't catch her breath and was hyperventilating, I thought she was having an asthma attack," Kaitlin told the *Los Angeles Times*. "It helps when somebody else slows down their breathing with you. . . . It was scary." Eads ended up being okay, and Kaitlin played a pivotal role in the frightening ordeal.

Things were looking up for Kaitlin in 2007. After such a strong performance at the Grand Prix, she finally went head-to-head with Yana Klochkova from Ukraine, her old nemesis, and defeated her. Kaitlin won the 200 IM at the World University Games in Bangkok, Thailand, winning in 2:12.13. Yana finished second in 2:12.16, yet another epic finish between the two elite swimmers. But this time, Kaitlin came out on top.

She didn't have time to dwell on the incident or any of her swims. It was back to Ann Arbor to continue preparing for the Olympic trials. Training was tough, but Kaitlin inched closer and closer to a third Olympics.

"I got a lot of confidence back in Athens," Kaitlin told the *Orange County Register*. "After everything I went through after Sydney, I lost a lot of confidence. I started to wonder if I was ever going to swim fast again." The challenge of the change of scenery took a toll, but she was able to fight through it and stay on track, remaining one of the world's elite swimmers. But being in Michigan was much different. It was cold and lonely for such an outgoing personality. Thankfully she had some friends on the team and also had visitors from time to time.

"I remember flying up to Michigan to hang out with her. We just always picked up where we left off," Amy Walloch said.

That was my first time ever going to Michigan. We went on a very cold, very snowy weekend. I remember her being super thankful. Living that far away from her family was so hard. She was swimming and working out all the time. She had this little dog. I remember thinking how much she was an adult with her own place, her dog, being a professional athlete. It was a nice break when we came because she felt like all she did was swim. We went shopping and went out for drinks and out to eat, just the normal things we would do if we were together. It was like giving her a little piece of home. She was definitely tired. And she had the injuries, especially the stress fracture in her back. It was her job.

And that job took a toll.

"When she was in Michigan, I saw her at meets. The sparkle just wasn't as bright. It was more getting to the end of her rope here. She was hurting, and that was clear. It was not that she wasn't working hard or trying," Rachael Waller said. "It was almost a passing of the torch. It was sad and bittersweet for her, but you knew she was ready to go on to the next phase."

It was something everyone started to pick up on, something that happens to every athlete, especially the world's elite.

"Every athlete goes through a tough time. She left 2004 on such a high note. You are on such a high and have done everything, I mean she broke a world record, where do you go from there? You are trying to take it to the next level at your own career," Diana Munz said.

> That would be winning individual gold. But you have four years in between, and that is a long, long time. And a lot of things happen, especially when you are getting older in the sport and the kids are getting younger in the sport, and you see that stuff on a daily basis. You are training with kids who are younger. They can bounce back from practice better. She was in Michigan, which is a totally different environment than California. There are so many factors that go into it that you don't take into consideration during the moment. You are looking around so much at the people training with you, and it can be really hard. I also think as you become more of an adult there are more things to worry about going forward, too. As a kid, you can kind of just do what you want to and it isn't that big of a deal, but at that point, she was a pro, she had lots of sponsors coming her way. There is pressure you have to try to avoid, and it is hard to do that. All Olympians, whenever that happens, your heart breaks for them because you know exactly what they are going through. You are at Olympic trials and have so many kids looking up to you. No matter what, it is harder when you get older. It isn't just your body, it is the responsibility on your plate, too.

But one more big finale remained.

With about two months remaining before the Olympic trials, Sandeno was optimistic. She had proven she could rise to the occasion in the past, and her competitive drive pushed her through two of the hardest swimming years of her life. There was a different confidence surrounding Sandeno in Ann Arbor. It was maturity, accomplishment, and drive all in one.

But the confidence was about to be shattered. It started with a simple knee strain but spiraled into a nightmare of ailments that would ultimately crush her dream of making a third Olympic team.

"Two months out from trials, I strained my knee pretty badly on a flip turn somehow," she said. "I was on crutches short term, not kicking, no breast-stroke, and even tried a cortisone shot for some immediate relief as trials was fast approaching. I pushed through only to get the sickest I had ever been two weeks before trials."

This wasn't a sickness that a few days of rest would cure, either. "I had a severe upper respiratory infection. I recall having a hard time just walking up the two flights of stairs to my house," Sandeno recalled.

My mom happened to be in town during this time and went to the doctor with me. I remember sitting in his office listening to his diagnosis and just knowing that this was the end of my swimming career. It was like a wave of disbelief, almost calmness, was rolling through me. I remember looking at my mom with tears in my eyes and a heavy heart. She kindly said that we could go back to California at any point. I didn't need to swim at trials. I told her I wanted to go to one more swim meet. I wanted to go out on my own terms. I wasn't negative, but I was realistic. I knew the 2008 Olympic Games wasn't in my future. But I couldn't just walk away after four years of incredibly hard training and not race just one more time. I wanted to know my last race, not have it taken away from me.

It was a difficult moment for Kaitlin, as well as her family. "It was hard to watch her go through that. You just want your kids to be happy and healthy. For so long we were just grasping at straws trying to figure out what was wrong," her mother Jill said. "When she was sick, I told her we could just go home now and not go to trials. We were all prepared for it being the end."

Then there was the issue of what swimsuit to wear. Kaitlin was sponsored by Nike but was feeling like she could be faster in a certain Speedo suit.

"That was the year of suit mayhem," Kaitlin said.

Nike was trying to be competitive in the race suit sphere, but our suit wasn't testing to be the fastest, while Speedo was. I loved being sponsored by Nike. There were so few of us, and they treated us so well. We all knew each other and traveled a lot together. I give Nike mad props because at trials, they told us to wear whatever suit we wanted. "You are a Nike athlete so wear your Nike clothes, but if you think you will make the team in a Speedo suit, then wear it. If you think you can make it in a Nike suit, please do." I was still on my antibiotics from my illness at trials, and my knee was still bothering me. I knew it was going to be my last race. I wanted to go out with Nike. They had been so good to me. They spoiled my family as well. We were so hooked up. I really wasn't going to make the team regardless of what suit I was wearing. That was me thinking realistically, not negatively. I didn't tell anyone what suit I was going to wear.

Kaitlin exiting the pool after winning at the 2004 World Short Course Championships in Indianapolis. *Peter H. Bick*

I took my jacket off and it was a Nike suit, and my Nike team went nuts on the pool deck. I felt proud to do that. They provided me with an amazing contract that provided an amazing life. I still have savings because of them. They took a chance on me.

Her sister Camlyn remembered,

Her last race. The whole bathing suit controversy. She was sponsored by Nike but had the option to wear Speedo. Nike told her to wear whatever felt best. She qualified for finals. We had a conversation about what she should do. I told her if this was going to be her last race, go out with a bang. Do the Nike suit. Make it to finals in the Nike suit. She was the only swimmer wearing a Nike suit. It was such a way to go out because they were so good to us. Standing ovation. Everyone knew it was her last race. They threw her a party. I was wearing a Nike red shirt with a flag. Kaitlin came into the room, and I started bawling. I have the best picture of her comforting me. She probably should have not swam, but she qualified and was emotional.

With nothing to lose, and knowing this was her final meet, Kaitlin made it a memorable one.

"I made it all the way through to finals in the 200 IM. Not sure how, but I did. I remember just having fun before it. Dancing behind the blocks with Amanda Beard. I touched the wall to see eighth place by my name and a very nonimpressive time," she said.

I looked at my family and remember them standing and clapping for me. No matter what, they were always my biggest fans. I immediately felt lighter. Like a huge weight had been lifted off my shoulders. I just sat in the water for a long time. Took my cap and goggles off, and just took it all in. I was done. That was my swan song. And I was ready to close that chapter. Natalie Coughlin swam passed me to get out of the pool and said, "I'm going to miss you." I was the last person to get out of the pool. As I walked off the pool deck, I was blown away by the standing ovation I received—and was even more surprised to get pulled aside by NBC to give what would be my final postswim interview. It was a very bittersweet evening. Tears of all emotions. The highs and lows and everything in between, and boy did I have my fair share of them all my lengthy career. And the crazy part is, I wouldn't have changed a thing.

That moment is permanently ingrained in Natalie's mind. There are many swimmers who end their careers, but there were few with whom Natalie had a bond like the one she had with Kaitlin. They grew up as competitors, swam some of the same events, went to rival colleges, and were Team USA members together, winning gold on one of the most epic relays in Olympic history. That is something you don't forget, or take lightly.

"So, Kaitlin's last Olympic trials was 2008. It was the 200 IM. It was her last race. She and I had such a nice moment. We had just swam the finals. I had somehow made the team, which still boggles my mind," Natalie said.

> She didn't make the team. We were exiting the pool, and she was congratulating me and saying all of these nice things. We were still in the water by the ladder. I remember that vividly. Then she said, "You know, Nat, I am so happy that my last race was with you. That was my last race as a swimmer." It is something that still makes me a little emotional, even now. It was so nice that we got to share that moment. It wasn't the outcome that she wanted, but she was able to go beyond herself and congratulate me. I just remember that moment. It was really sweet and really special.

It was emotional for her coaches, too, seeing the end of a career they helped begin.

"We were at the trials. We took our whole family out there and got to see her last meet," Vic Riggs said.

> I wouldn't have expected anything less. She was really struggling at that point physically. But she still qualified for finals. To get up there and swim in a Nike suit, they told her she could wear whatever. It was a classy way to go out. Swimming was not who she was, it was part of what she did. I don't know when the realization came to her, but she handled herself with grace and left the sport that way, which doesn't happen very often.

It was a sweet and special moment for her family, as well as her friends watching around the country.

"We were at my parents' house, and we knew she was sick and hurt, and we were hoping and praying she would be able to overcome everything," Kammy Miller said.

> I remember watching on TV how gracefully she spoke and how humble she was in her retirement. To watch her get out of the pool and be interviewed on deck after her last race, and speak so eloquently about her career, was a proud moment as a friend. To be able to handle that with grace and dignity was a cool thing to watch. As sad as you were for her in that moment, you knew more was coming. That is when I saw her start to get a bigger voice.

The end is never easy for an elite athlete, but it is also a challenge for those around an athlete. Kaitlin's family and friends were extremely supportive; however, it was still bittersweet watching the finale for those closest to Kaitlin—even if they were in a competing lane.

It turns out, Kaitlin wasn't going anywhere. She would always be around the pool and end up doing more good in the world after her swimming career came to a close.

"She was disappointed not making the team, but she was ready to move on. She was more than a swimmer," Urbanchek said.

> She didn't want to be known just as Kaitlin Sandeno the swimmer. She had so much going on in her life, which we can really see right now. She does a lot of work on the dry side, especially with the Jessie Rees Foundation. She is known throughout the U.S. for what she does for this cause, which everyone can identify with.
>
> She has name recognition because she deserves it.

That name recognition allowed Kaitlin to have as much success in the next phase of her life as she did in the water. She just had to wait for the right opportunity. It led to another—and another—as she found her role giving back to her sport and her world.

10

PLENTY ON DECK

One of the most difficult aspects of starring in a sport that relies on an Olympic cycle is not falling into oblivion once it is over. Many swimmers are household names for a couple of weeks every four years and then immediately forgotten about as focus shifts back to mainstream sports. Swimming has increased in popularity, with athletes like Michael Phelps, Ryan Lochte, Missy Franklin, and Katie Ledecky remaining in the public eye and staying relevant, and social media has a lot to do with that.

When Kaitlin Sandeno concluded her swimming career after the 2008 Olympic trials, there was no social media and no way to remain relevant without being in the public eye constantly, which most people can't do, or at least don't want to do. In fact, many swimmers enjoy being able to go back to relative obscurity after finishing their Olympic careers. Kaitlin was happy to be done swimming but wanted to remain relevant in her own sport, as well as maintain the platform Olympians have to try to continue to give back and be a positive role model.

Kaitlin made plenty of rounds with speaking engagements, endorsement engagements, and other commitments. "I toured the country for some time representing GlaxoSmithKline and speaking about asthma awareness," she said. "That's when my passion for using my platform for a healthy lifestyle first began and when I gained more knowledge about asthma. I loved being able to encourage people with health issues. Not letting their obstacles get in the way with having a healthy and active lifestyle."

Her desire to use her platform only increased when it came to the Jessie Rees Foundation. "When I met Jessie Rees and her father, Erik Rees, I knew right away I wanted to get involved with encouraging children fighting cancer to Never

Ever Give Up," she said. Sandeno was so connected to the Rees family and the foundation that she became the national spokesperson for the charity. "Becoming the national spokesperson was absolutely life-changing," she continued. "For the first three years, I was on the road a lot, meeting and encouraging many kids and families. Each time was truly a priceless experience. I can honestly say with my 160-plus visits, it never gets old. I feel honored to continue what Jessie started."

Having someone as outgoing and well known as Kaitlin within the sport is something the foundation couldn't have found anywhere else. Former coaches and teammates alike have found the same sparkle in Kaitlin's eyes that they once saw after a triumph in the water a constant presence as she has continued her post-swimming passion.

Her friends understood how special the foundation was to Kaitlin but didn't fully get it until they saw her in action giving out JoyJars at a hospital visit.

"We went to Chicago to visit Bree [Deters] for her birthday," Rachael Waller said.

We got to do an actual hospital visit with her. It is great to see her passion in it. You wanted to watch her swim because of the passion and emotion she put into

Klete Keller, Rachael Waller, Bree Deters, Vic Riggs, Kaitlin, and Erik Vendt.
Sandeno collection

Kaitlin's NEGU family, Cory Tomlinson and Shaya Rees, showing off the NEGU gear co-designed by Sandeno. *Sandeno collection*

it. She is the same way with the Jessie Rees Foundation. She got me into it. At my company, you can pay $5 to a charity to wear jeans. We do that for the Jessie Rees Foundation. You can see how much she wants to help kids, and it is contagious. She is trying to give these kids just a little distraction from their everyday pattern. When I actually went to the hospital with her, I had heard about it like a thousand times. She was visiting hospital after hospital. The strength that she has to be able to work with these kids is amazing. It moved me in a way that I didn't think was possible. They don't deserve to be in the position they are in. Just seeing their faces when she pulls out her medals is a really touching thing to see. It took me a little bit before I felt comfortable interacting. The energy in the room is so different. It was tough for me. The kids are just excited to see you. It gives them an opportunity not to think about how sick they are. Some kids have siblings there visiting, too, and you have to think about how it affects them, too. She pays attention to the sick child but also their families. She talks to everyone. She creates this environment where she is just engulfed in it.

But it is the kind of passion that made Kaitlin such an elite swimmer in the first place.

"I am not surprised she has done so much after swimming. It is the kind of person that she is. She is just a really good person. She really cares about people. She loves her sport. She loves children, and the Jessie Rees Foundation is her heart," former coach Renee Riggs said.

She has probably gotten more out of that than anything she has ever done. She is the perfect ambassador for that. When I think about how difficult those hospital visits are constantly, she is in there bringing those kids joy and is smiling the entire time, it has to be difficult. I am so proud of what she has done.

While Sandeno's face was appearing throughout the country for a variety of different causes, she was eager to get back into her sport in some capacity. Little by little, she found her way back in a variety of ways. She is a youth swimming coach in her hometown and remains on the national stage, doing swimming commentary for NBC and USA Swimming, as well as being the on-deck emcee for the Olympic trials.

"In 2014, I had an awesome experience being the play-by-play commentator for the youth Olympic Games. Being on set at NBC and in the booth with the headset and microphone brought me back to my longtime desire of wanting to be a sideline reporter," she said.

The 2016 Olympic trials in Omaha, Nebraska, was literally one of the best weeks of my life. Although not in the water, my role at this trials was incredible. It was such a rush to go live every morning of trials for their web series and every evening for finals as the arena emcee alongside Brendan Hansen. The adrenaline kept me up at night. It was such a high. Trials is so electric and so full of energy that being a part of it was absolutely amazing. I literally ran on no sleep, tons of coffee, and the energy of the arena, but I would do that every day of the week if I could. I had the time of my life. It was so exciting to interview the Olympians just qualifying for the team. Felt so full circle, once being in their shoes. I felt like I could really connect with the athletes, giving the audience a better glimpse into this swimmer's true personality.

It was a familiar path, one that one of Kaitlin's role models, Summer Sanders, had taken after winning gold in a successful swimming career. In fact, when Sanders interviewed Kaitlin during her final Olympic trials, she asked Kaitlin

Kaitlin interviewing former teammate and friend Michael Phelps after he made his fifth Olympic team at the 2016 trials. *Sandeno collection*

what she would like to do after her career. All smiles, Kaitlin responded she would like Summer's job. It was not intended to be prophetic, however, as answering the question in the heat of the moment simply showed what Kaitlin was really looking for.

Once she realized that was the direction in which she really wanted to go, she sought out Summer. "She is a lot younger than me, so we weren't ever in the pool at the same time, but I obviously watched her career, which is fun—watched it transition into TV," Summer said.

> I am always just so proud when a swimmer transitions into something they love. Taking the leap and going into television and things like that. It is just a completely different perspective in a sport like swimming, where you are judged on her time. I just feel a kinship with her. I started commentating in 1996, then went into the NBA. I remember one of the first times meeting with her was her asking for advice. I love when athletes have the guts to ask about getting into TV. I love the idea of influencing younger swimmers.

She also kept her face out there as a part of USA Swimming's *Deck Pass Live* show. "It was surreal timing. After my honeymoon, I had just started coaching. I remember getting an e-mail from Mike Unger of USA Swimming, wanting to get in touch. He said they were looking for someone to interview swimmers on the pool deck, and they thought I would be great for it," Kaitlin remembered.

> I was like, "No way!" I was so honored to be asked. As we got closer to trials, they said they were going to try something new called *Deck Pass Live* that had a college football *Gameday* vibe. I loved it. My role ended up much bigger at finals, being the emcee. I had the time of my life doing both of those roles. I was on an adrenaline rush the entire time. I really enjoy interviewing athletes. I love engaging with them, not so much about times or numbers, but getting to know them and bringing that out. I had been trying to put myself out there more and rebrand myself. I didn't swim when there was social media so I kind of had to restart that brand. A lot of kids didn't know my swimming credentials. It is branding this new identity. I am just really blessed that USA Swimming keeps asking me back. You have to find your niche. I know I am great talking with athletes. But talking tempos and stroke rates is not necessarily my jam. I enjoy spicing it up and bringing some different entertainment to the sport when I am hosting.

It was an opportunity for her friends and family to see Kaitlin in a different way.

"I was on the fence about going to the trials. It was in Omaha and I live in Chicago, not that far. But when I heard Kaitlin was hosting it, I wanted to go and support her. It was really fun to see her back in her element," Bree Deters said.

Kaitlin on deck at the 2016 Olympic trials. *Peter H. Bick*

A lot of people with profiles like that act like it. But everyone knows her. Every-one wants to talk with her. She is just so good at it. It was fun to see her back in that element, then get to hang out and hide out with her. A lot of the kids there weren't even born when she was swimming at the Olympics. We were laughing about how a lot of them called her "host girl." We were part of her entourage, but she is grateful for every opportunity and brings those close to her everywhere she goes. It is not her thinking she is so popular that she can force her entourage into a party. She has a celebrity profile in that community but still likes to keep her people close. But she doesn't do it at the expense of people that she doesn't know. She signed so many autographs. She kept apologizing to us. I am so biased to Kaitlin because I have known her for so long. When I introduced my boyfriend to her, he was like, "Oh my gosh, you know an Olympian?!" and I am like, you know it is just Kaitlin. Now, he gets it.

Everyone who meets Kaitlin gets it, and thanks to her second phase in the swim-ming world, more people continue to get to know her.

"I was honored to have been asked to fill those two roles at trials and have the absolute best memories of it," she said. "After I was done competing in 2008, I felt like I needed a good, long break from the sport. I didn't really follow the sport or attend the events. But the youth Olympic Games and then the trials refreshed my love for the sport and a niche I absolutely love being in."

And it isn't the only niche, either.

"I loved hosting the stuff on the pool deck in Omaha," Summer said.

I longed for a connection to swimming. I think most of the kids had no clue who I was, but it was a fun moment for the parents remembering back to their day. That was really fun for me. I am just so proud that Kaitlin has had the guts to venture out and do other things. With that comes recognition, and that is amazing. They long for success in another form. That is the true success. It is awesome for her to be recognized as a swimmer and someone who is making a difference in the world. The guts to ask for advice shows the vulnerability you can show even at the top of your game in life. Her passion is what you need to be successful. It means enjoying the next phase of life. The name might get her into a meeting, but she needs to bring her game to that meeting. That is what I love about her story.

"I love [watching her emcee the trials]. It is totally her," Diana Munz said.

It is exactly what she should be doing. The Jessie Rees Foundation is exactly what she should be doing. She makes so many people smile, and it is the perfect fit for her. She really is that bubbly girl. You want to see someone who knows their stuff, knows the sport and has that personality . . . it is huge.

Kaitlin also turned to coaching, where she coaches a team similar to the one on which she started in Lake Forest. She is still part of the Jessie Rees Foundation and has about a thousand other things she is involved in.

Kaitlin and Natalie Coughlin were brought together again in 2018, as captains for a USA Swimming team competition at the pro series events, the equivalent of Fantasy Football for swimming. They were two of the four captains.

"For me, I have been telling people swimming with me that we should have been doing this since 2004, having participated in Fantasy Football and that it inherently makes you care about athletes you wouldn't normally," Coughlin said.

My grand plan was to have a fantasy swim league, and maybe the winner could win two tickets to the Olympics or the trials or something. So, a decade later, Lindsay [Benko] Mintenko, with USA Swimming, approached me, and with it giving our charities publicity, it was a win-win for me for sure. It was fun. Definitely the first four picks were pretty straightforward. But after that, it was a little different. I had only been out of swimming at that level for less than a year, and there were plenty of people I didn't even know. Kaitlin has been out of swimming for a lot longer. It was fun when we got past the fifth round. At that point, it was like blindly throwing darts at a dartboard. Between the four of us, we were only together at Golden Goggles for the draft. You could tell who did a lot of homework. You can tell that Lenny Krayzelburg plays a lot of fantasy sports. We definitely trash talk. I was trash talking the entire time. That is what makes fantasy sports so fun. And the best thing is everything goes to charity. It is win-win for everybody.

It was just one more way for those faces to be there for the sport and for one another. Kaitlin has been doing things both in and out of the sport since she retired as a competitive swimmer.

"When I first was done swimming, I was consulting for Nike. I would go to different swim meets to try to get teams to be Nike teams," she said.

I also started working at Think Physical Therapy, working on stroke technique for athletes in their pool at the clinic. We filmed them underwater to watch their stroke technique. You came to improve your technique or see what you were doing to cause pain while you were swimming. That is when I started working with Ella Eastin.

Eastin, who would go on to set several American records and win a handful of NCAA championships at Stanford, quickly remembered everything Kaitlin did for her at ages 11 and 12.

"We came to know each other in a few different ways. We are both from the same area. Through some mutual friends and my physical therapist, I ended up getting to meet her and do some stroke instruction with her," Eastin said.

They had a swim lab in the back of my therapist's office. I decided I would benefit from talking with her and [learning about] her experiences. Her career and different processes with college and the Olympics. I wanted to learn from her success and failures in a personal way to be able to keep them in my back pocket. She was always so supportive of me. She was a really good mentor. I met with her frequently and worked with her every once in a while. I was on the junior board of directors at the foundation. We kept in contact. Luckily with social media we are able to see what each other is doing all the time. She did swim some of the same events that I do. I was really able to connect with everything she talked about. We both had shoulder injuries, and there were a lot of parallels there. It was an incredible experience having someone I looked up to take interest in me.

It is that interest that makes Kaitlin so vital to so many different groups of people.

"I was also a varsity assistant coach for a prominent private high school in our area, Mater Dei, while I was working at Think PT. Then I met the Rees and started my role in the Jessie Rees Foundation," Kaitlin said.

In 2015, right after I got married, I took over the summer league swim team in my hometown, 200-plus swimmers ages three to 18 years old. I have always done

Kaitlin's last season coaching her nephew and niece,
Max and Sarah. *Sandeno family*

speaking engagements—that is one of my favorite opportunities I do—and a little
bit of modeling here and there. Then having such a big role for the 2016 Olympic
trials has led to similar roles on the microphone with live audiences. When my
mom got sick, I took time away from everything but the swim team to be there
with her. It was a blessing that I was able to take that time to be with my mom.

Somehow, even with everything that was going on in her life at the time,
Kaitlin found time to fall in love.

"I had gone over to Camlyn and Steve's house in January 2013. I was turning
30 that year," she recalled.

My sister made a comment that she knew I was going to meet someone this year.
Rewind a month before that. End of December 2012. I was getting massage treat-
ment from Liz Freeman. She is a small-in-stature woman, from Great Britain.
She climbs on top of you to get all your aches and pain to dissolve. She is a huge

energy person. She has every kind of client. She always asked who I was dating. She could always feel my energy and would say she knew I wasn't into someone. She was waiting for a right time to set me up with someone, but we were both in relationships. She went on and on about this Peter Hogan. She said he had more of a Colorado vibe although being from Newport Beach and played football in college at CSU. We joked I wanted a tall guy I could wear heels with, so he would be perfect. He sounded so great. But at the same time, I had never been set up on a blind date before. She called him right away. She gave him my number and told him to call. Christmas came and went, and I kind of forgot about it.

Middle of January, it was the NFL's AFC and NFC championship games. My phone rang. I saw that it was a Newport Beach number, but I couldn't believe he would call on a football day like that. Sure enough, it was him, and he leaves me the cutest message. I called back, and we set up a time to get together for dinner. I

Mermaid vibes, mermaids being Kaitlin's favorite mythological creature. *Don Le*

wanted to go in open-minded. I didn't want to see what he looked like beforehand or anything. We went to dinner, and, of course, I did most of the talking. I was excited afterward, but it wasn't like, oh yes, I have met "the one," but I definitely wanted to go out again. We went on our second date, which led to a third and so on. In March, I went on a girls' trip to Chicago, where Bree, Rachael, Amy, and I celebrated St. Patrick's Day/my birthday, and while I was there I realized I was in love with this guy. I tried to talk myself out of it because I couldn't believe I could fall in love so quickly. It had only been two months! When I got home, he took me to the beach and told me he loved me. I started laughing because I couldn't believe that he felt that, too. The rest is history. Erik Rees married us, and Liz rang the wedding bell at our wedding service. He completes me in the perfect way. He is mellow and soft-spoken but is very engaging. He balances me so well and brings out the best in me.

Pete quickly thought the same thing.
"I met Kaitlin through a close friend, Liz Freeman," Pete said.

Liz had been my masseuse at the time [and still is], and she had been working with a handful of swimmers. I remember Liz bringing up Kaitlin a number of times, but at the time I was in a relationship and Kaitlin was as well. A couple of months later, when my relationship ended, Liz made it very clear that Kaitlin was single. She didn't hesitate to give me her number and said it would be foolish not to call her. About three months later, after a visit with Liz, I gave in and finally called her. I remember it was on a Sunday in January 2013, right before a Green Bay playoff game. I left a message, and she immediately called back. I am not the best on the phone, so it was short but sweet. We set our date for the following Thursday, and not only did she sound great, but she was on her way to a party to watch the game. One box checked there—she likes watching football.

They connected and met for a blind date.
"We decided to meet at a central location, so we met at Houston's Restaurant, which is halfway between the Balboa Peninsula and her place in Irvine. I was looking forward to the date all week, but it was my first blind date so I was nervous," Pete continued.

She was beautiful at first sight. Leading up to the date, I had only seen the pictures Liz had shown me, along with the photos I'd seen online and on Facebook. Kaitlin was high energy, and there were no moments of awkwardness, partly because she was smiling and laughing the entire time. If you know Kaitlin, you know her loud laugh—a great laugh, but can be heard by all in a 30-foot radius. Time flew at dinner, and we stayed there and talked for well over two and a half hours. We were both leaving town the following day, and I left wanting to see her again and hoping she felt the same way, too. The entire next week we texted and followed up with a date the weekend we both got back into town.

It wasn't long before her family was convinced that Pete was there to stay.

"Tom and I think he's perfect for Kaitlin; therefore, he fits in perfectly with our big family. He 'deals' with Kaitlin really well," Jill said laughing.

Our grandchildren love him. Steve [brother-in-law] and Pete shouldn't be left alone together [total trouble makers]. I think he is sweet but has an adorable mischievous side. He's hilarious; dry but quick. Low-key and subtle. He doesn't need an audience, not looking to be center of attention. He's "Sweet Pete" in my phone contacts. He calls me MIL [mother-in-law], and I call him SIL [son-in-law]. I enjoy football season with him. And he's always cute when Kaitlin is away and we can watch her online. He sends me texts like, "She nailed it!" He's a proud husband.

Tom has a great relationship with Pete as well and has been impressed with how his son-in-law approaches life, especially from the standpoint that he can be in the background at times when Kaitlin is in the spotlight.

"He's an all-around good guy with a great personality and a humor that is Pete," Tom commented. "I think guys were intimidated by Kaitlin, but it doesn't affect Pete that Kaitlin is in the limelight from time to time. He's confident and secure. He's very warm to all our grandkids. Comes from a great family, and we are grateful they live so close."

It didn't take long for Kaitlin's friends to fall in love with Pete, either.

"She told me about him before they even met," Amy Walloch said.

She told me about the massage therapist setting them up on a blind date. I have been around a lot of boys with her over the years. But after date one, she was a smitten kitten. I feel like they are the yin and the yang. He is a calming force that really grounds and balances her. She is this ball of energy and light. Not that he isn't, but he just balances her out. He is quiet but not at the same time. I love what he has done for her. They are just so great together. He is so supportive of her, and that is very comforting for me as a friend. Men can get very proud and macho. But she is clearly the one that is kind of famous and the one everyone knows. It doesn't bother Pete one bit. He is so happy just being with her and being by her side. He is a chill dude.

"To me what was so unique about it is that she always approached dating kind of cautiously," Bree Deters said.

It took her a while to really open her heart up. But with Pete it was 100 percent different. As soon as they met it was completely different. He came to trials and he was so starstruck. "That is Michael Phelps, oh my gosh!" Kaitlin was like, "Pete you are embarrassing me." She wasn't always looking for a significant other, but she just knew right away with Pete. It took her a little later than typical to meet him, but he was completely worth the ups and downs to get there. Over the years, there have been trends of accepting who she is and also trying to separate. I think that is a natural thing for any person of her caliber of an athlete to struggle with. Now, the pendulum is swinging more toward owning her past instead of separating completely. I think that is one of the things that drew her to Pete. He said over and over at trials how much he loved seeing this side of her because he never had before. He was getting a taste for that part of her life because he didn't get to experience it. He really loved that.

"I really enjoy watching swimming, so I really enjoy going to the events and watching the best in the sport compete," Pete said.

I always enjoy going to swim events with Kaitlin and seeing her old coaches and teammates. Yes, I do get starstruck by Olympic swimmers, about as much of the same as I would as a NFL athlete. Meeting swimmers like Nathan Adrian, Michael Phelps, Jessica Hardy, Jason Lezak, [and more] at the events has been an enjoyable experience. Even though I wasn't around for it, I am so proud of her swimming career. I have always enjoyed watching swimming in the Olympics, so I know I watched and rooted for Kaitlin in 2000 and 2004, not knowing she was going to be my beautiful, loving, loud-laughing wife. Swimming is my favorite way to work out, so not only do I respect swimming athletes, but I love the sport myself. Going pro in your sport is one thing, but going to the Olympics and winning four medals is a whole other level. She can honestly say that during her career she was one of the best swimmers in the world. Her career was nothing short of unbelievable.

But he has enjoyed getting to know post-swimming-career Kaitlin even more. "Kaitlin is a very confident but humble person, so she doesn't need to introduce herself, expect to be recognized, or to be acknowledged as an Olympian," he said.

Sometimes when I am looking at Kaitlin, I step back and think, my wife's an Olympic medalist—crazy. Meeting Kaitlin has changed my life for the best. She is so positive and supportive, and I feel our personalities mesh so well. She is high-energy, and I would call myself mellow and more introverted. She has definitely helped me come out of my shell and grow into the man I am today, who is way more confident than ever before. It's no surprise that she was raised by an awesome family.

Kaitlin and Pete's wedding day. *Sandeno collection*

It wasn't long before Kaitlin and Pete were married. The ceremony took place on April 25, 2015.

"Our wedding day was fantastic," Pete said.

We got married at a traditional church in Corona del Mar. The service was perfect for the two of us. The wedding ceremony was intimate and embodied what we are all about—family and friends. After the ceremony, my parents' best friends were kind enough to take us by boat to the afterparty at the Newport Harbor Yacht Club on the Balboa Peninsula. We took a lap around the harbor and enjoyed the moment. The weather was imperfect, cloudy and rain drizzle, but perfect for us because we love the rain, and come to find out that is better for the photos. Once we got to the club, the drizzle had subsided, and we were greeted by the entire group at the dock as we walked in. We enjoyed a wedding like it should be . . . we danced all night to the best band in Orange County, the Tijuana Dogs. The night ended at the Blue Beet with more dancing. It by far exceeded my expectations.

One of Kaitlin's favorite wedding pictures, with friends looking on in joy. *Don Le*

Kaitlin and Pete at their wedding, which Kaitlin refers to as the "best night ever." *Don Le*

The fact that our relationship grows stronger the more time we spend together tells me that our relationship has a solid foundation. Kaitlin is perfect for me in that she is everything a partner should be—supportive, loving, and aware of my strengths, weaknesses, and aspirations. I am proud to be Kaitlin's husband because of who she is. I envision us laughing, dancing, and holding hands well into our 90s.

While building that love and bond with Pete, Kaitlin has also seen her faith grow. She was not a very religious person growing up, but her faith has grown in her as an adult. Her oldest sister, Amy, has a strong faith, and that connection—the same connection that was always tough to foster because of the age difference as kids—has grown abundantly as adults.

"Faith is something that bonded us," Amy said.

It has been an interesting journey being her older sister, but I feel so lucky to have her as my sister. Your family is forever. Whether you realize it or not, they will always be there for you. My son James' birth was very traumatic. My uterus ruptured, and they had to do an emergency c-section. I started hemorrhaging. The next day, I forgot I had a baby. I was in the hospital for a week. I literally remember hearing internally someone tell me Kaitlin will be the godmother. She was not baptized at that point. Shortly after that, I get a phone call, and it was Kaitlin wanting to become a Christian. She started seeking out her faith. With what happened to James, she said she stopped doubting. She was baptized the week before James was baptized. I will always remember that in the hospital. It was really shown to me that this was going to happen.

It isn't just her connection with James, either. When another nephew was having trouble fitting in after a move, it was Aunt Kaitlin to the rescue.

"I love the fact that she is younger, so she can relate differently. She has that impact to help speak some sense into the kids. They respect her, and she is fun. I love to see her interaction with those kids," Amy said. "Thomas had the hardest time moving. My entire family rallied around him, and Kaitlin came to the rescue and talked to him and told him things that I couldn't. She gave him an action plan. Now he is probably one of the most popular kids there."

Kaitlin's faith is not something she flaunts, but it is also not something she shies away from, making her an easy person to have a conversation with.

"We were the family that went to church on Christmas Eve and Easter. I always believed in something, but at the same time, I had questions also," she admitted.

It wasn't until I was in Michigan and in a relationship that I started to get more curious. He was strong in his faith but was very patient with me; he didn't force it on me but was always willing to share or answer my questions. He had the best demeanor about it. He didn't push it but was confident, secure, and proud about it. He went to church, and if I felt like joining him, I would. I started going with him to be a supportive girlfriend, but then I had even more questions. He was like, "Well, just ask me." I really appreciated that. I still appreciate that to this day.

After I was done swimming, my godson James was born. My sister was in labor with James, and I still wasn't really sure what I thought about religion. I joined a women's bible study. It was at 9 a.m. on Tuesdays, and I was the youngest in the

Tom and Jill Sandeno with Kaitlin and Pete. *Sandeno family*

group by like 40 years. But I really enjoyed it. I went with a really good friend of the family, Carol Benson, and I just listened and took it in. Then my sister was going through her delivery of James. She had a very tough delivery. Crazy things happened. They were really nervous for Amy's life and James' life with the complications that happened. Amy came out strong, and James came out strong. Amy is a strong Catholic. The doctor made a comment to my sister that more than just his hands were in there today, and he left it at that. But it was definitely something we picked up on. I felt a really strong bond to James when I met him and got to hold him. I remember I had to leave for an appearance and was really emotional because I didn't want to leave. I wanted to stay with my sister and James. I remember holding him in the hospital thinking he was a miracle. How could I question that? It was almost like everything kind of came to light for me in that experience. Then Amy asked me if I would be his godmother. I was so honored. Because it was a faith thing, they wanted their godparents to be baptized, which

Kaitlin and her godson, James, have built a special bond, which has included Kaitlin coaching her nephew. *Sandeno collection*

makes sense. I was talking with her about it. She wanted to make sure she was not pushing me into this, but at that time, it was something I really wanted to do. I wanted to do it even more because of James. I was baptized on Easter and then became his godmother. Ever since that moment, I have been strong in my faith.

Kaitlin has started to attend church on a regular basis, something she is able to share with the rest of her family as they have grown together.

"I don't go to church every Sunday, but we go quite a bit. For me, going to church doesn't define faith. But I enjoy going to church. I feel really peaceful there," she said.

[Mount of Olives] is a Lutheran church, and my dad's grandfather was actually a Lutheran minister, so I guess it was always in our blood. I believe everybody gets to their walk of faith on their own. It is such a personal journey. It is something I can always grow in and improve upon, and talk with others about when it makes sense. The thought crosses my mind that I would have loved to have my faith during my swimming career. I really think it could have helped me, but I also believe there is a reason for everything and everything is in His time. That is my biggest thing. He is in control, and I always try to lean on that. I would rather my actions speak my faith, more than my words. I respect everyone's walk that they are in faith-wise. It is so amazing with the Jessie Rees Foundation. It is faith-laced. There are a lot of strong Christians.

It was huge for our relationship. It took us a long time to have things to bond over because of our age difference. I always felt better knowing Amy was praying for me or our family. Now Pete is a godfather and I am an honorary godmother to his godchild, and take pride in being my youngest nephews' godmomma. I have a few beautiful cross necklaces I love wearing, one from Pete and one from my parents. I have a small cross tattoo [along with my Olympic rings]. It is subtle. I'm a proud Christian, and I hope my actions speak my faith.

"Probably the most profound impact on her after her career was her faith journey," Kammy Miller said.

She is a person of great faith. It is super important to her. It created a new foundation for her. Maybe before swimming was her foundation, actually family was. It was just a new page in the book of Kaitlin. After she was baptized, that opened her eyes to a different platform that she could have to give back, helping give voices to people who don't have them. I have been on hospital visits with her. I have seen that impact she has. She is captivating. It doesn't matter if she is being watched or not, she is just as captivating. The work that she does is intensely satisfying, as it is for anyone who has a chance to give back and see an impact—to have a chance to see someone smile when they are at their physical worst, and probably their emotional worst. To be able to, in just a minute, bring a smile to someone's face has had a profound impact on her and strengthened her faith. It is a cool thing to watch. To have the platform she has and bring awareness to helping kids just want to smile is a really cool thing that she gets to do. The more I see her speaking, and at the last trials, that was really cool. I was there watching every day. Her voice has gotten louder, and I don't mean that in a decibel level. Her voice has grown exponentially. She has always been really confident and been an eloquent speaker.

It isn't surprising that Kaitlin is there for her family at every turn. That is who she has always been. It is the way she was raised. But it doesn't stop with family.

"She is the kind of friend that if you call her, she will be there," Rachael Waller said.

My cat was dying, and she came up. I told her she didn't have to, and she said, "I know I don't, but I will be there in an hour." I wanted to stay with my dying cat so I had to miss my family Thanksgiving for the first time ever. She insisted on not only coming to her family's Thanksgiving, but I packed up my cat and stayed with her for the weekend. I couldn't have felt more welcome. I was so sad about my cat and missing my family Thanksgiving. It really touched me.

No matter what the people closest to her are going through, Kaitlin wants to be part of it, no matter how busy she is. It is the mark of a true friend.

Kaitlin at her home pool, where she has swum and coached. *Dan D'Addona*

"I moved to Chicago in 2009 and then came back to Southern California for a year. When I came back, I started going through a period of depression, and she was there all the time for me," Bree Deters said.

> She swooped me up. We started hanging out a lot more. She completely absorbed me back into her life. She was the reason that I became okay with the decision that I made to move back—just by being a good friend. She got an offer to be a celebrity on a celebrity cruise. All she had to do was talk a few times. Famous chefs and famous football players. It was for her and a plus-one. At the time, she was dating someone, but it wasn't serious. I hated my job at the time, and it was a three-week cruise. She convinced me to quit my job and go on this three-week cruise with her. It was a once-in-a-lifetime opportunity. We sailed from Ft. Lauderdale to Europe: the Azores, Lisbon, Paris, Dover, Amsterdam. We just laughed the whole time. The next-door neighbor would tell us he could hear us laughing at four in the morning.
>
> People didn't believe she was one of the celebrities because she just talked to everyone all the time. She joked around with everyone and was so down to earth. It was so fun roaming around Europe and doing this. We shared a bed for three weeks straight. The last night of the cruise, we realized that those beds, you can actually separate so it is two twin beds. It took us three weeks to realize that, and we just laughed and laughed. She is one of the only people that makes my stomach hurt from laughing every time I see her. She has these amazing things happening—she attracts these amazing opportunities to herself.

And she shares them. It was a typical laughfest, as Kaitlin is accustomed to having with friends, but the selflessness behind the smiles and laughter is what sets her apart from others.

"It is not surprising to me because I know her as a person," Amy Walloch said.

> She is just such a giver. Seeing her in these roles is just what she was made to do. She owns it. She is so great at everything. I couldn't be more proud of her. I have gone with her to do some of the hospital visits. Seeing how she is with the kids is so nice. She is just so genuine. No matter how much fame or fortune she got, or will ever get, it will never change who she is as a person. To see her be able to touch other people is thoroughly inspiring. We are in our 30s, and we start to question things. Am I doing enough? Am I giving back enough? I just started tutoring because I needed to do something. She found her calling, and she is so amazing at it. She is a light, and everyone is drawn to her. Not that she doesn't have down times. I have seen plenty of that, too.
>
> One of my bosses had a daughter that was swimming and was getting really frustrated, and I asked Kaitlin to send her a note of motivation or an autographed picture or something. She ended up flying out here and speaking to that swim

club. They had a meet and greet. It was amazing. She is just so willing to share her story. I love that she is vulnerable enough to share her struggles because it has made her who she is. I remember her having her injuries and not thinking that she could do it anymore, and being tired and wanting to give up. Turning that in to an opportunity to let other people know she is human and has ups and downs. She kind of takes it and perseveres with it. I think it is amazing.

Many people know how important of a figure Kaitlin is in the swimming world; however, many younger swimmers don't realize that she was one of the most versatile swimmers in the history of the sport.

Every Olympics has a face of swimming, both male and female. It has been Michael Phelps for quite some time on the men's side, but on the women's side, there has been a passing of the torch like few other sports have seen in the past 30 years. From Tracy Caulkins to Janet Evans to Summer Sanders, the sport progressed from the 1980s through the 1990s. When the Olympics returned to the United States in Atlanta in 1996, it was Amy VanDyken who almost surprisingly joined that group. Between Van Dyken in Atlanta and the current face of swimming, Katie Ledecky, there was Kaitlin in 2000, the teen sensation heading into Sydney, although Brooke Bennett and Misty Hyman had better Olympic performances. Kaitlin returned and was joined by Natalie Coughlin in 2004, as Coughlin won the 100 backstroke and teamed with Kaitlin on the epic 800 freestyle relay that closed the meet with the breaking of a previously unbreakable record. Coughlin gave way to the comeback of Dara Torres, then another teen phenom in Missy Franklin, before Ledecky began her dominance.

Because there have been so many faces of the sport for the U.S. women, there is a special bond and camaraderie they share. It is something they don't really talk about, but there is an understanding about what it means to be in that group.

"I remember being a spectator at the 1984 Olympics, and to me Tracy Caulkins and Mary Key were like the queens of all queens," Summer said.

This is what is so amazing about the sport of swimming. You are all a part of this same family, and you never really forget each other. Even when you get older there is this kinship. I don't know if you find that in every sport. As you become more of a veteran you do become part of that, and it is extended from generation to generation. They see the leaders before them and are put in that position or decide to be in that position and take over that role. It is not a chore, it is an honor. That has been a longstanding, important part of United States swimming.

"I think it is really important for alums of the national team to stay close to the sport," Natalie Coughlin said.

It has been so refreshing to see what Kaitlin has been doing. She is made for doing that emcee work. She has the energy for it, and she is amazing at it. You see a lot of swimming alums leave the sport and never come to any meets or Golden Goggles. I get that to an extent because life is busy, but it gets a little sad when you lose touch with everyone. I think it is great what Kaitlin has done. She has given back to the sport that has given her, and me, and all of us so much. I think it is really important. We, as Olympic athletes especially, are given a platform for giving back. I always align myself with charities that mean something to me personally. What Kaitlin has done with NEGU has been great. When she speaks for that, it is obvious that she speaks from the heart about it. It is not some script that someone has given her, and I think that makes a big difference.

Kaitlin worked for 15 years in the pool to create that platform. In fact, she created her own path that is focused on others.

"It goes to her character as a person," Vic Riggs said. "To see a kid that you have known for so long dedicate themselves to something so important . . . it is like, 'Wow.' She never lost that desire to have a multipurpose life. To watch that grow has been pretty fun. Everything she dips her fingers into is something special."

Everything.

From participating as an emcee at big meets, to coaching a youth swim club, to hosting a USA Swimming television show, Kaitlin has kept her voice and spirit alive in her sport and maintained her platform. But even more important has been what her platform has accomplished.

Kaitlin's true impact lies in what mark she has made on others, from her own family to complete strangers. Whether it be coaching her nieces and nephews, speaking about asthma, going on hospital visits with the Jessie Rees Foundation, or just holding her mom's hand before a radiation session, Kaitlin's ability to bring a smile to everyone in her presence is what makes her so special—and what allows her to help everyone find a silver lining and change it to gold.

ABOUT THE AUTHORS

Dan D'Addona is a writer and editor for *Swimming World Magazine*. He has covered swimming at every level since 2003, including the NCAA championships, USA nationals, Duel in the Pool, and Olympic trials. He is a native of Ann Arbor, Michigan, and a graduate of Central Michigan University. He is also is sports editor at the *Holland Sentinel* in Holland, Michigan, where he lives with his wife, Corene, and daughters, Lena and Mara.

Kaitlin and Dan begin the process of collaborating for this book at the 2016 Olympic trials. *D'Addona collection*

Kaitlin Sandeno Hogan is an American former competitive swimmer, Olympic gold medalist, world champion, and former world record holder. She is also the national spokesperson for the Jessie Rees Foundation, a well as a motivational speaker, coach, sports commentator, emcee, and host for world-class sporting events. She lives in Orange County, California, with her husband, Peter.